# Sales 3.0
## The New Cont@ct Sport™

How to Use and Leverage
Social Media Marketing for
Small Business Sales Success

**By
Doug Dvorak
CEO DMG International**

# Praise for Sales 3.0 The New Contact Sport™

"If you want to learn the secrets of how to promote your business on the internet using social media marketing, then read this book".
-Ken Wyrick, CEO, KLW International

"Successful, useful social media marketing advice from someone who understands what it takes to excel in business today".
-Roger Dawson, author, Secrets of Power Negotiating

"With intense competition in today's business environment, Dvorak shows you how to get more traffic to your website and more customers to your business by implementing their incredible and cost-effective Social Media Marketing Strategies".
-Jean Pierre Boespflug, VP Cisco Systems

"Sales 3.0 The New Contact Sport demystifies why some people succeed while others fail in business. I've seen, heard and read a lot of Authors and Internet Marketing Consultants on the subject of Social Media Marketing and none capture this hot topic like Doug Dvorak".
-Paul Sheedy, Director Ernst & Young Consulting

"As the result of implementing Doug's Social Media Marketing strategies, I have blown away my sales quota and doubled my income with less stress."
-Scott Lindblad, Sales Manager, JC Penny Incentive Sales

"Wow! Dvorak takes you on a magnificent journey through the digital marketing universe. This is a must read for anyone who wants to take advantage of the latest and most relevant Social Media Marketing tools and strategies".
-Russ Herriges, Founder & Principal, Herriges Creative World Wide

"This book should be required reading for marketers – or anyone who wants to navigate the rapidly changing and evolving digital marketing landscape".
-Mike Breen, Vice President of Business Development,
The Sales Coaching Institute

"Sales 3.0 The New Contact Sport teaches readers how to win the search engine wars and create an effective on-line digital brand through Social Media Marketing".
-Wolfgang Salb, Managing Director, WAS Development Corporation

"This book changed the way I viewed traditional marketing. I will never again purchase another print ad or radio/TV spot. Dvorak helped me to understand Social Media Marketing and I've never looked back. My site traffic is up over 1500% and sales have never been better".
-Mike Kozar, Vice President of Sales, Crosscom International

# Sales 3.0
## The New Cont@ct Sport™

How to Use and Leverage
Social Media Marketing for
Small Business Sales Success

by

Doug Dvorak – CEO Digital Marketing Group

Doug is the Author of the books

Build Your Own Brand,

The Masters of Success &

101 Motivational Mantras for the
New Millennium

The Big Book of Sales Solutions

501 Sales Ideas to Win More Business

## Doug Dvorak
Doug founded the Digital Marketing Group in 1998 after leaving Worldnet Corporation for which he was Senior Vice President of Sales and Marketing. With a background in sales, marketing and Internet technologies, he began to develop, discover, and adapt new ways of leveraging results-oriented, creative social media marketing techniques to help small businesses increase sales.

# What's Sales 3.0 The New Cont@ct Sport™ about?

**Sales 3.0 - The New Contact Sport**™ guides small-business professionals, salespeople and anyone seeking to harness the power of social media marketing to access specific markets and to target certain demographics. In the face of tough market conditions that only get tougher with each passing day, this book can be a survival guide for any entrepreneur or small business. Entrepreneurs running smaller businesses will learn how to create a driving force for growth with a well-developed social media marketing plan. This book shows the reader about every aspect of social media marketing and identifies the potential of sales success in consolidating as well as expanding business.

**Sales 3.0 - The New Contact Sport**™ teaches real world methods of social media marketing and their application to businesses and professionals. By using the methods and tools in this book, a reader can easily create a successful sales strategy for their small business and carve a niche in the market in an inexpensive and productive way.

Written in simple language, **Sales 3.0 - The New Contact Sport**™ encourages readers to practice the techniques explained and outlined in the book. Within a few hours, a person or an organization can start building a sturdy, successful small business.

# Sales 3.0
# The New Cont@ct Sport™

## Table of Contents

Foreword
1. Introduction
2. Why Social Media Marketing and Why Now
3. Social Media Marketing – The New CRM Solution for Small Business
4. Seven Deadly Sins of Social Media
5. Blogging for Small Business Success
6. Facebook
7. Twitter
8. Linkedin
9. Video (You Tube, Animoto, etc.)
10. Social News
11. Best of the Rest – (Yahoo, Flickr, etc.)
12. Social Media and Search Engine Optimization
13. Social Media and Online Reputation Management
14. Measuring Social Media Marketing Success (Web Analytics, Google Analytics, etc.)
15. How to Increase Website Conversions
16. Conclusion
17. References
18. Bibliography
19. Links Index

# Foreword

## By
## Roger Dawson

This is the book that I'd been hoping someone would write ever since social media like Facebook and Twitter came out. I knew that connecting with friends and clients through social media would be essential to my future success but I couldn't understand it.

To promote effectively via the social Web, you need a knowledgeable guidebook – this is that guidebook. My good friend Doug Dvorak touches on the marketing issues of social media, and then lay out a systematic approach to putting together a social media marketing plan customized to your small business.

The book is well written, well organized, and full of content.
By the time you put it down, you'll be an expert. It has 16 chapters split into sections that are easy to understand and follow. I love the summary sections at the end of each chapter. I read them before reading the book and it gave me a great overview of what was to follow and a much better understanding of the content.

If you want to tap into the power of the Social Web through connected networks and consumer-oriented media, this is the book you need as a "roadmap" to help you build your company's social media marketing plan.

Roger Dawson
Author of Secrets of Power Negotiating

Twitter: @RogerDawson

Web site: www.RogerDawson.com

# Chapter 1

# Introduction

# Introduction

Effective and efficient sales and marketing practices for Small Business should now be centered on the new and evolving methods known as Sales 3.0 and Social Media Marketing. In the wake of emerging websites such as Facebook, Twitter, YouTube, Linkedin, and other social media marketing platforms and sites, these effective and free technologies are changing the landscape for Entrepreneurs and small businesses around the world. Thus, as small businesses begin to realize the benefits of these free and wide-reaching tools, sales and marketing efforts can be improved for better results.

**Traditional sales and marketing methods for small businesses**
Older methods of sales and marketing have seen a decline in effectiveness and use of budget. Snail-mail, in-person prospecting and phone calls are becoming an inefficient and ineffective use of small businesses capital and resources. Either by direct costs or the time it takes for the owner or sales people to perform these duties, the cost efficiency of such endeavors are undermined. And for these methods to be successful, they must incorporate high standards, which is costly. However, as reported in a USA Today online article (22 June 2010) on viral advertising, Russ Klein, Burger King's chief marketing officer states that "People have grown increasingly skeptical of packaged, canned, Madison Avenue-speak." Truly these ineffective ads that take budgeting money away cannot be the focus of small businesses.

**Benefits of Sales 3.0 tools**
As small businesses are introduced to newer Sales 3.0 and social media marketing tools, the general inefficiency of traditional sales and marketing methods are much improved upon. The first thing Sales 3.0 and social media marketing tools improve upon is in regards to direct advertising costs. Small business owners are discovering the power of these tools, and for a much lower cost than traditional means.

These newer methods can be obtained for no cost. And if money is to be spent somewhere, these networks and tools represent smart options for the time and resources invested. In the second instance of improvement using Sales 3.0 tools, manpower is saved. Time wasted by the sales staff in regards to traditional methods is remedied. They can now focus on utilizing these networks and tools, thus cutting time spent with ineffective traditional methods.

It is important that small business owners recognize the effectiveness of such tools and technologies. By using and leveraging certain social media marketing websites, tools and online networks, millions of people can be reached, especially on the Internet.

In an article featured in the New York Times (online 10 July 2009), David Appelbaum, vice president for marketing at BigFix explains a marketing initiative run by the company: "'Forty-five percent of the Web traffic to our main corporate site was originating from the viral campaign' last fall, he adds, and it is 'still driving traffic.'" In the article, Mr. Appelbaum reported that the campaign generated 400,000 customers. Like BigFix had experienced in the New York Times article, similar results can be obtained for small businesses with effective Sales 3.0 and social media marketing tools and campaigns.

**Reaching your target market free and effectively**
It is important for small business owners and entrepreneurs to realize the staggering audience that can be reached with Sales 3.0 and social media marketing. Social networks are an excellent example: according to statistics found on the social networking website Facebook, it has over 550 million active users. Other networking sites such as LinkedIn and Twitter reach millions of users across the globe and have become paramount for sales, marketing, advertising and brand enhancement. In national and local markets, small business can expand their reach and exposure, through the use of social networking and Internet communities. Enthusiasts with reviews, advice, and forums can be found dedicated to a virtually unlimited amount of industries and products.

**Activity and exposure**
Small business owners and entrepreneurs should ensure that their sales and marketing efforts remain active and fresh within social communities and opportunities. It is important to establish a level of rapport within the community. Members cannot be blanketed with advertising attempts. When possible, demonstrate how to offer advice, get to know members and tastefully introduce others to one's product or business. Other slightly different online services can be effective for small businesses in any location. Linkedin, Digg, Propeller and StumbleUpon represent unique opportunities in Sales 3.0 and social media marketing. These websites allow for a great deal of exposure based on the popularity of a website. At no cost, pages can be placed on these websites. If users find them useful or entertaining, your pages could generate a great deal of exposure and profits.

**Sales 3.0 and social media marketing opportunities**
Sales 3.0 and social media marketing represent a unique opportunity that can transform a small business. While these tools and communities offer excellent paid

advertising prospects, they can be effectively utilized for free. When small business owners consider this with the audience, exposure, and new business opportunities that can occur, they are excited about the unlimited potential for sales and marketing success.

As Sales 3.0 and social media marketing tools and opportunities can offer vast improvements over traditional methods, small business owners should consider blending these to utilize the advantages of each. The sales and marketing opportunities available for small businesses on the Internet are reshaping their marketing world.

**Sales 3.0 and social media marketing - the next sales frontier**
Technological innovations have always influenced and changed the way we live. Buying and selling, formidable facets of life, also get transformed by the latest developments in technology. Technical developments such as the advent and the growth of the Internet have created value for both buyers and sellers alike. Sales 3.0 and social media marketing is a term coined to reflect the usage of WEB 2.0 and other technologies that expedite marketing and sales success for small businesses.

In simple terms, Sales 3.0 and social media marketing means nothing but the usage of the latest technologies to leverage sales and meet buyer needs. The latest web technologies and social media form a part of Sales 3.0 tools. Sales 3.0 approaches produce superior, predictable, and repeatable business results. They can cut costs, save time and sustain a competitive edge. Sales 3.0 is still the same age old concept of sales, only the process and methods have evolved. Sales 3.0 concentrates on engaging customers and developing brand loyalty with the ultimate aim of driving more sales.

**It starts with a website**
To reap the benefits of Sales 3.0 and social media marketing processes, a small business needs to have a website and preferably a blog. A website is on 24/7 and can be accessed across the globe. A website can describe and define a small business in finer details and at times can serve better than a sales person. Interested people can receive regular newsletters from the website and be updated about the latest development concerning the product or services being offered.

A blog will declare to the world the latest developments and different perspectives about a brand. Interested people can post their queries or comments. By answering their queries, sellers can clarify doubts. Responding to comments the sellers can bring potential buyers closer to the knowledge about the ability of the product or service to meet their needs.

**Techniques of getting traffic**
Simply having a website is not enough. The website must get traffic to obtain a favorable ranking by Google, Yahoo, and other search engines. Search engine optimization (SEO) techniques and getting linked to other websites are an indispensable part of the web 2.0 process, which in turn is a part of the Sales 3.0 and social media marketing process. In addition to having content rich with search engine friendly key words, your website and blogs should be linked to an RSS aggregator. Your blog also needs to be a member of Technorati, the blog-ranking search engine.

**Using the Internet to promote your brand and sales**
Many businesses that use Sales 3.0 and social media marketing techniques embed audio and videos of products and brands on their websites. They broadcast clippings of their business videos on websites such as You Tube. Sharing visuals greatly enhances visibility of the product or service. You can also create buzz for your product, such as Nike's campaign with Kobe Bryant "jumping a car" to promote its' new shoes. The video became a viral sensation.

**Social media marketing savvy**
Your business or you should have profiles on various social networking sites such as Facebook, Linkedin, and Twitter. Sales and marketing techniques have improved with the evolving behavior of buyers. If seven or eight years ago buyers loved to spend time chatting on Yahoo or MSN, now they prefer to keep in touch with friends and associates as well as make new contacts on social media. Networking in social media spheres helps increase sales directly. The CBS Interactive Business Network (BNET) reports that interacting with a prospect on a social media site increases the likelihood of getting an appointment by eight times.

We all know what its like to make or receive cold calls. Sales people would love it if the awkwardness of talking to strangers could be eased a bit. Establishing some rapport with people from an organization would help a great deal in picking up the phone and making the call. Social media marketing helps in creating familiar grounds. Being a part of the social media world enables businesses to get a chance to feel the pulse of the buyers and the market trend. Businesses might even be able to position themselves to influence market buzz. These aspects of being social media marketing savvy are definitely going to help your sales and marketing efforts.

## Sales 3.0 is all about speed

With the help of technology small business owners and sales reps are now able to close deals at a speed that was not possible a decade ago. They get messages through instant messaging or SMS about the latest moves of the prospects. It is now possible to have a feel of the pulse of the prospect constantly enabling you to close the deal when the prospect is hot. Accessing emails on mobile phones and replying to them is one of the technological advances that help.

Sales 3.0 and social media marketing is still about human relationships. Technology has only modified the process and the end result remains the same. Sales 3.0 and social media marketing is not a transitional phase after Sales 1.0 and before Sales 2.1. It is an effective sales and marketing tool. Sales in the next decade will be steered by Sales 3.0. Those entrepreneurs and small businesses that are not using it should embrace this new model of sales and marketing. You will be amazed at the results!

## Chapter 2

# Why Social Media Marketing and Why Now

# Why Social Media Marketing and Why Now?

Ask Sam Whitfield and Kristi Cunningham how Social Media can change the whole dynamics of a ubiquitous business model and propel it to new peaks of success. The duo changed the course of their respective careers as a lawyer and business consultant in August 2009 and launched Curbside Cupcakes, a mobile gourmet cupcake company. The business clicked, literally, and now is a sweet success!

"Looking for an evening cupcake treat? We'll be parked outside the Sackler Gallery at about 8:30PM. Come see us!" Tweets like this announced where and when their mobile van would arrive next. The mobile vendor of gourmet cupcakes smartly utilized Twitter and Facebook to connect with its potential consumers.

The success story of Mission Pie is equally enterprising. "HEY first peaches of the season are here. Come and get your peach pie @10am." Simple tweets like that have helped the sumptuous store serve its mouth-watering array of sweet and savory pies. "It tends to have a sort of street credibility, which traditional media lacks," quips Krystin Rubin, Mission Pie's co-owner. She reckons Twitter deserves much of the credit for her success.

Power of Social Media Networking: Not only entrepreneurs, but politicians are also discovering it

Tech-savvy politicians and opinion makers are fast jumping on the Social Media bandwagon by prominently using popular networking websites to reach out to masses and supporters. The idea is to establish a link with supporters and prospective voters by leveraging reach and power of the Internet. The medium is cost-effective, compared to TV, radio and print, they believe, and rightly so!

Social Networking sites have become important vehicles for news and influence. During Barack Obama's rise to the Presidency, he gathered 5 million fans through Social Media Networking. About 5.4 million people clicked on the "I voted for Obama" button on Facebook. Importantly, his Social Media campaign resulted in three million online donors raising $500 million in funds. Both Twitter and Facebook played a starring role in the online campaign strategy that helped sweep him to victory. During the Presidential election, Barack Obama proved to be something of a trailblazer in using Social Media tools to get his message out and rally support. This is an apt illustration of the growing power of Social Media and how, if applied effectively, it can deliver astonishing results.

It is no surprise then that even small businesses and not just the big boys now have Twitter accounts. Its popular counterpart Facebook facilitates small businesses to undertake targeted marketing, which could not have been possible a few years ago. Facebook users provide information like age, location, occupation, religious beliefs, activities and interests, favorite books and movies in their profiles. Companies are tapping into this information to understand the social behavior of their potential audiences as well as to deliver messages to the relevant target groups.

Let's now look back at the early days of Social Media for a better appreciation of its origins and ambitions.

## A quick peek into Social Media's past
*We are social animals for whom networked software is creating a new kind of habitat. Social software can be defined as whatever supports our actual human interaction – new media innovator Jon Udell*

Sir Tim Berners-Lee in his book "Weaving the Web" mentions that the Internet was always meant to be more of a social creation than a technical one. He notes that the ultimate goal was to come up with something that would make it easier for people to collaborate with one another. From its very inception, the Internet and its predecessors like the Arpanet and bulletin boards have been the focal point of social interactivity.

The Internet was initially envisaged as a military scheme but it slowly expanded to entertain ideas about connecting computers to create a forum for discussing topics of mutual interest and to meet old friends as well as seek new acquaintances. Its evolution into a Social Media tool began in the 1970s with the Bulletin Board System (BBS). CompuServe, which allowed members to share files, access news and events and most importantly, send e-mails to each other along with America Online (AOL) that offered member-created communities and member profiles, were the genuine predecessors to today's popular Social Networking sites.

Classmates.com pioneered a new model of Social Networking in 1995. Former Boeing employee Randy Conrads created it with the idea of locating old school friends for a virtual reunion. By the mid-1990s, Yahoo and Amazon had entered the fray. On the other hand, BlackPlanet.com and MiGente.com followed SixDegrees.com and AsianAvenue.com. By 2002, Social Networking had gained real momentum with the launch of Friendster soon followed by networks like MySpace, Facebook, Cyworld, Orkut, LinkedIn, and Twitter.

## Social Media Marketing: Optimization and trends
*Engagement is all about making it relevant to the consumer – Andrew Miller, Ernst & Young CEO*

Social Media Marketing is now considered an integral component of organizations' integrated marketing communications plans to connect with their targeted markets. It helps organizations by providing a reliable channel for customer support, a means of gaining customer insight, and a method of retaining their competitive edge online. It's a relatively new arena of marketing that small businesses still find a bit daunting. When Citibank polled 550 small business owners across America in an April 2010 survey, it found that most of them did not utilize Social Media to promote their products or expand their business, despite the fact that social Media has already evolved into the mainstream.

Conversely, certain tech-savvy enterprises are using corporate blogs and Twitter updates to launch their Social Media strategy. These also allow customers to learn about new products and enable customers to immediately address their concerns and questions. Such initiatives are helping many small businesses to expand at little or no cost with very small budgets. According to a study by research firm MarketingProfs, this has helped improve the company's reputation with the amount of negative blog posts dropping from 49% to 22% since the start of the site.

Social Media Marketing (SMM) is aimed at increasing the awareness of a brand, product or event by using Social Media outlets to generate viral publicity. SMM includes utilizing social networking sites; social news and bookmarking sites; RSS feeds; business promotional sites; as well as photo, video and blogging sites. SMM is quite similar to Search Engine Optimization (SEO) in which the ultimate goal is to drive targeted traffic to your site.

In the following pages, we shall discuss various kinds of Social Media Networks and the factors that underscore the growing importance of using Social Media to attract and hold potential consumers' attentions.

## Different types of Social Media sites
*There are hundreds of Social Media tools available today that can help organizations to achieve their business goals and objectives.*

Facebook is the world's most popular Social Networking site in terms of worldwide active users. In January 2009, it overtook MySpace, which concentrates primarily on music, as the most popular social site. However, the latter remains strong in the US. Orkut, owned by Google Inc, has not gained a foothold in the US, but remains one of the most visited Social Media sites in countries like Brazil and India. Twitter, as we all know, allows members to send 140-character messages called 'tweets'; Twitter began as a micro-blogging site but is fast evolving into a social messaging platform.

These sites boast a variety of technical features like photo-sharing (e.g. Flickr) and video-sharing (e.g. YouTube) capabilities, built-in blogging (e.g. Blogger) and instant messaging applications, thus attracting a wide range of users. Some are built specifically for mobile-users (e.g. Dodgeball), though a few Web-based avenues also support limited mobile interface (e.g. Facebook).

Top networking sites outside America
Most countries like Germany, Russia, China, and Japan boast local players like Tuenti in Spain and L'Internaute Copainsdavant in France as the most visited Social Networking sites. According to comScore, among top international Social Networking sites are Russia's Vkontakte, Belgium's Netlog, Japan's Mixi, and Berlin-based StudiVZ. In China, 51.com and chat conglomerate Tencent QQ are the more popular Social Networking sites. Other most popular sites in the world include Ning, Skyrock (France), Passado (France, Spain and Germany) and Cyworld in South Korea.

In Finland, the Saluke-owned Habbo was launched in 2001 as a network for musicians but has now been transformed into a major Social Networking site aimed at teenagers. Habbo's success is fueled by its user interface where users can operate personalized avatars to visit virtual hotels and make new friends. Users also get currencies (called Credits and Pixels) to purchase furniture and effects for their virtual avatars.

StudiVZ, started in 2006, is the most visited Social Networking site in Germany and other German speaking countries like Switzerland and Austria, says a Nielsen study. The Belgian networking site Netlog is the second most visited site in Belgium, Austria and Switzerland—behind Facebook.

Niche networking sites
While most Social Networking sites are promoted with the aim to build a mass base as quickly as possible, some sites cater to a specific audience.

Specialized sites often find an enthusiastic following as they have the advantage of quickly connecting people with similar interests and having a larger and influential voice within a niche social network. Amongst the most popular targeted sites is

LinkedIn, which helps people boost their careers through professional networking.

Social Networking has also moved into the corporate world with networks like Yammer, Lotus Connections and Chatter allowing internal knowledge sharing. There are several smaller Social Networks that appeal to specific interests like Piczo (aimed at teens in the US and Canada), StudiVZ (for German students), Muxlim (for the world's Muslims) and ResearchGATE, a scientific network. Then there is Athlete Focus for action sport athletes, Fuzzster for pet lovers, Yub.com for shopping freaks, Model Mayhem for models and photographers, Mog for music lovers, and Artybuzz for artists. There are sites based on religious affiliation, political view, sexual orientation and other specific categories. Even pets have their own Social Networking sites like Dogster.com.

Many of these sites tend to attract their initial constituency from a particular geographical or linguistic group, age or education level. Over time, they embrace a wide variety of users. Orkut's success in Brazil is a good example of this.

Some analysts contend that niche social sites are a natural outgrowth of the popularity of sites like MySpace and Facebook. Conversely, there are people who would prefer a smaller, more personal experience and turn to niche sites. These typically begin with a small base and then grow quickly but the growth plateaus after sometime, because there are only so many people to fuel the growth.

Enterprise 2.0 networks: New Media for the corporate world
Businesses may use both closed and open social networks to share information and communicate with their customers. Closed networks foster communication and knowledge sharing, as well as encourage ideas that would otherwise be lost within a larger organization.

Corporate networks also open up direct lines of conversation between the company and the customers. Amazon-owned online retailer Zappos has developed a Social Media and customer integrated business model and encourages employees to use social networks. Many others are using them to inform customers about new services and answer questions about their products.

Enterprise 2.0 networks like IBM's Lotus Connections, UserVoice and Chatter from Salesforce.com, built for the corporate world, work on the same principle as Twitter and Facebook. UserVoice is another corporate networking platform. It allows companies to focus on their customer base and capture their feedback and ideas without installing complicated software.

Such micro-interaction and the emphasis on customer service create word-of-mouth buzz, which ultimately translates into customer loyalty.

**Harnessing Social Media for business success**
Social Media has become one of the most important marketing trends for advertisers. Companies are increasingly turning to it to provide primary awareness for their business and are reducing their spending on traditional advertising channels.

Research by mobile-phone operator O2 found about 17% of the UK's small and medium businesses surveyed were using Twitter to attract new customers. Most of them were able to enjoy significant savings in marketing and recruitment costs by using Social Networking services. Another study, carried out by Penn State's College of Information Sciences and Technology, scanned through half a million tweets for keywords and found that about 20% of tweets mentioned specific brands or products.

Small and medium businesses use social networks to create and promote blogs, presentations, white papers, branded groups and communities. Indeed, creating a social forum and encouraging discussions about the product between potential customers and the team is essential. For example, Seattle-based bag manufacturer Tom Bihn uses online forums, blogs and Facebook to communicate with fans, as well as Flickr and YouTube to show off its unique styles. Social networks are not only helping to promote existing businesses, but also to build new business models like Zynga and Playfish that run popular online games on these sites.

The power of Social Media Marketing lies in its ability to allow small businesses free access to their audience and a level playing field to market their business. Steve Hasker of Nielsen Online says that social network services have created the world's biggest, fastest and most dynamic focus groups, proving to be a boon to aspiring entrepreneurs with light budgets.

<u>What makes Social Media one of the most dynamic tools of marketing?</u>
Let's explore some aspects that make Social Media one of the smartest and most dynamic tools of marketing today. It can be treated as a form of Internet marketing that aims to achieve branding and communication goals through activities that integrate technology, social interaction, text, images, audio and videos in various Social Media Networks. They essentially are web-based services enabling individuals to build a public or semi-public profile that include details like age,

location, occupation, religious beliefs, interests, favorite books and movies in their profiles.

Advertisers are tapping into a wealth of information so they can understand the social behavior of their potential audiences as well as deliver messages to relevant target groups. Social Media Networks enable advertisers to add demographic criteria and keywords to check the number of users that fall into their target audience.

In essence, social network marketing has dramatically altered the way a business can be marketed and communication can be established with both existing and prospective customers.

People now spend more time on social networks
Cordarounds, a small American clothing company, is a great case study in utilizing Social Media efficiently. After spending time on Twitter, employees noticed that many folks twittering in their area were using bicycles to get to work. So the company produced a new line of trousers, dubbed 'bike-to-work pants', with built-in reflective materials – making wearers more visible to traffic while cycling at night. The company resorted to tweets to spread the word about its new product line, and the results were astonishing.

Social networks create a very powerful viral marketing effect. They allow businesses to undertake targeted marketing that was thought to be beyond the realm of possibility just a few years ago. How has this transformation happened?

The leading market-research firm, Nielsen, reckons that people have started spending more time on Social Networking sites than on e-mail, and the gap is only getting wider. While most social network sites may employ key uniform technological attributes, they cater to a wide and diverse range of audiences.

A recent study by mobile measurement firm Ground Truth, found that approximately 60% of the time spent on the mobile Internet is consumed by Social Networking sites and applications. Users spent only about 14% of mobile Internet time on portals, the second most popular category. It also revealed that mobile-centric Social Networking sites such as MocoSpace and AirG – which are chat-based platforms - have higher consumer engagement levels as compared to platforms like Facebook and MySpace, designed primarily for PC access.

Social network users' recommendations influence purchase decisions
"The whole point of Social Networking is that its users determine what they want

it to be: They can be as edgy or as square as they want - it's up to them." This observation by the co-founder and chief executive of MySpace, Chris de Wolfe, sums up the spirit of Social Networking.

Two-thirds of all purchasing decisions are influenced by word of mouth mostly taking place on the web, says a McKinsey report. People tend to believe their friends' opinions more than advertisements. Savvy marketers understand that recommendations of social network users are an important vehicle in influencing purchase decisions. Popular social networks accelerate this process, for instance, by automatically alerting an individual's friends when one signs up to become the follower of a particular product or brand on a site.

A recent Nielsen report finds that ads in the social space are more effective than other ads. Jon Gibs Vice President of Media Analytics for Nielsen Company says, "It's critical we not only understand advertising in terms of the impact of paid media, but also in terms of how earned media and social advocacy impact campaigns."

Once people's interests are aroused, they pass the information to their friends and connections, fueling a viral loop of awareness. Consider the case of Casemate, which turned an innocuous product like the 'recession case' into a sales leader. Initially skeptical about the practicality of the product, the company got in touch with blogger Larry Greenberg who posted an article about the case. Within hours, every major technology site like TechCrunch and Mashable picked up the news. The story spread virally and people shared it with friends and family, the company's Facebook and Twitter traffic skyrocketed. As a result, four days later, over 7,000 recession cases were sold.

Such successful Social Media campaigns prove that people are willing to engage with brands through social networks.

## Future of Social Media
*The "new influencers" are beginning to tear at the fabric of marketing as it has existed for 100 years, giving rise to a new style of marketing that is characterized by conversation and community - Institute for Public Relations*

The Los Angeles-based, Kogi BBQ, was conceived to cater to late night partiers who craved greasy snacks. Kogi, which has several trucks serving a unique combination of Mexican and Korean tacos, now has over 52,000 followers on Twitter and uses the service to tell customers where they can find its vans each day.

There is much public discourse about the future of Social Networking – is it a fad or a concept loaded with unlimited potential? Social network sites were not conceptualized for business. Rather, they were designed as communication devices and web applications to meet the growing 'consumerization' needs of information technology.

The Economist in a research report points out that social networks are more robust than their critics think, though not every site will prosper: "Social Networking technologies are creating considerable benefits for the businesses that embrace them, whatever their size." Analysts and observers believe this could be the precursor to an "exciting new era of global interconnectedness" that will spread ideas and innovations around the world faster than ever.

Geo-networking apps: The next big thing
The growing popularity of smartphones and their GPS capabilities can dramatically change the way people interact through Social Networking sites. Geo-networking applications, which use virtual data to connect users with local people or events that match their interests, is sure to be the next big thing in Social Networking.

Online geo-networking sites target locally familiar content leading to increased personal interaction between users in or around local spaces. Start-ups like Foursquare and Gowalla are building businesses around this idea. They use the GPS technology in a user's smartphone to spot their exact location, alert friends to their presence and provide information about events and happenings around them.

The growing usage and penetration of mobiles has made companies realize the importance of connecting with potential customers at a localized and personalized level. Microsoft has already introduced a line of mobile phones with Social Networking features. Twitter recently turned on its GPS feature that offers users the option to include their GPS location from each tweet. Facebook's geo-location feature is intended to let its users share their location with friends.

Corporate Social Networking services are for the future
Corporate networks are changing the communications landscape because employees now have tools that allow them to collaborate with colleagues and friends both within and outside the company. Companies are already registering obvious benefits of using Social Media Networks. They are able to gather and manage employees' ideas and knowledge to make better decisions and to become more productive.

Also, constant engagement with customers is helping several companies identify ideas and suggestions that impact customers directly.

Marc Benioff, Chief Executive of Salesforce.com, says that corporate Social Networking will get underway once managers realize that they now know more about strangers on Twitter and Facebook than they do about the people in their own organization. Benioff considers social computing to be the next big thing for the IT industry after cloud computing.

Franks Gens, Senior Vice-President for Research at tech market research IDC, says that while social software is perceived by many to be at the fringe of most large businesses, it has already become a vital tool for companies because "it's about how the next generation of employees communicate, create and share ideas."

Mobiles: Next growth driver for Social Networks
While mobile Social Networking is still in a nascent stage in several countries, it is expected to become a mainstream activity within the next few years. In a survey of 18-to-24-year-old users in the US, mobile consultancy M:Metrics found that 33.2% use their mobile phones to post photos to online sites as opposed to only 18.7% playing downloadable mobile games. The exponential growth in mobile adoption across countries will fuel future growth in Social Networking. Market research firm eMarketer estimates that over 600m people will use their phones to tap into social networks by 2013.

A recent study by Nielsen/NetRatings found that about 45% of active web users have logged onto Social Networking sites. While Asia and Africa still lack fast PC-based Internet connections, they will benefit from cheaper mobile broadband services. Some emerging countries have more people using cell phones than computers to connect to the web – opening up a new audience. Mixi, one of Japan's largest social networks, already draws a large chunk of its traffic from mobile customers. According to Facebook, mobile users are almost 50% more active than non-mobile users on it.

**In conclusion:**
Collaboration and convergence is the crux of communication today. Social Media networks are the new-age intermediaries between audiences and organizations that can initiate conversations, build trust, forge lasting relationships, and script success stories for budding businesses.

Social Media is about holding a conversation between people who share mutual interests. It is a collaborative process through which information is created, shared and discussed. Creating genuine interest among the people about a product is an important factor in using Social Media Networks to bring in sales.

Next Read: How Social Media is making CRM affordable for small businesses?
The next chapter will highlight how CRM strategies can:
- Help even small companies to increase value from existing customers and reduce the cost of supporting and servicing them, increasing overall efficiency and reducing total cost of sales;
- Improve sales and profitability by focusing on the most profitable customers and dealing with the unprofitable ones in more efficient and cost-effective ways;
- Support cross-selling of other products by highlighting and suggesting alternatives or enhancements;
- Implement enhanced and more effective targeted marketing communications aimed specifically at customer needs.

# Chapter 3

# Social Media Marketing
# The New CRM Solution for Small Business

# Social Media & CRM

A company's Customer Relationship Management (CRM) strategy is a framework that allows it to identify, attract, satisfy and retain profitable customers by managing effective relationships. This allows the company to focus on building lasting relationships by giving only profitable customers financial and social benefits to achieve increased profitability. With significant directional changes in marketing strategies over the years, marketers have learned to focus on CRM and ignore customers conducting individual transactions for reasons like increased competition and short product life cycle among others.

A sound CRM policy needs to be incorporated into a company's business and marketing strategies so as to yield better results. A CRM strategy pushes a company to focus on long-term profits rather than just acquiring customers for a single transaction to earn a little profit. It encourages the company to focus spending on providing better service to profitable customers to create a loyal customer base in order to ensure long-term profits in the future. CRM also advocates retaining profitable customers as the retention of existing customers is more cost effective compared to attracting new customers. Many firms today do not have a retention strategy.

CRM is not a new concept but its use has certainly increased during the past decade, especially with the advent of Social Media. Social Media has changed how small businesses look at CRM solutions. CRM utilizing Social Media Marketing has evolved and morphed into a customer-centric philosophy that must permeate every small business. It's a small business success strategy to be used to learn more about customers' needs and behaviors in order to develop stronger relationships with them.

CRM used to only be available to large corporations with big budgets, but the advent of Facebook, Twitter, LinkedIn and YouTube has changed the CRM landscape. Social Media marketing has offered companies a cost-effective way to communicate with customers as well as offered healthy insights into consumers, which improves customer service. Social Media has also made it easy to conduct cheap and cost-effective transactions, to research market trends and it promises better responsiveness between companies and their customers.

Social Media has indeed made the CRM process more effective and customer-friendly. The profusion of Social Media has improved customer service, added cross-sell and up-sell opportunities, improved close rates, streamlined sales and marketing processes, improved customer profiling and targeting, reduced costs, and has increased share of customers and overall profitability. The most appealing part of CRM using Social Media is that it provides small businesses with a voice and a public venue to monitor and respond to customers' needs, wants and desires in greater depth faster than ever.

**Identifying Profitable Customers**
Every company's CRM strategy has the grand ambition of identifying and retaining profitable customers. It is the driving need of today's competitive market. But it is not an easy task to achieve. However, Social Media networking sites have made it possible for companies to collate much data about customers, which can be useful in identifying repeat customers. A centralized database of customers facilitates easy administration as well as making it easier for companies to respond to queries and feedback. With Social Media, you can profile customers according to their sales behavior and product history to assess their future value.

It is important to ensure that a customer identified as profitable immediately gets routed to the service and sales department. A customer's history and buying pattern can also alert sales personnel about when and to whom they should try to sell a specific product or when to desist. Similarly, customer behavior data can alert sales personnel about a non-profitable customer and thus, ensure that they do not spend too much effort and time in influencing purchasing behavior. Another way to retain profitable customers is to provide them with attractive deals. When engaging a repeat customer, you can take a call on providing an individual pricing offer. Careful and efficient implementation of a system based on customer behavior can drive a successful CRM strategy.

The Right Approach
According to CRM marketplace analysts, the two common mistakes made by marketers when considering CRM are 1) assuming that acquiring a sound CRM technical solution is the most important step and 2) thinking that CRM is just another project, which is achieved once the goals are accomplished.

CRM is an ongoing process of managing customer relationships using a blend of people, business process and technology. If handled well, this synergetic blend will allow organizations to improve their ability to get, keep and grow profitable customers. Technology should be treated as an enabler that can help an organization to improve business problems, but it is not the only answer to such problems. Before embarking upon your CRM strategy, it would be best to identify your strengths and weaknesses when it comes to customer relationship management. Understand the issues within your marketing, sales and customer service departments and try to solve quickly. Remember, a successful CRM strategy is all about the people. Having a satisfied customer base is the starting point for maximizing your revenues and profits. To create loyal customers, you must have loyal and satisfied employees. Customer satisfaction will be the key differentiator in a competitive market.

**So what is Social CRM?**
Social CRM can be defined as a process that engages customers in effective communication to build a mutually beneficial relationship between a company and its customers in a transparent business atmosphere. Social CRM leverages Social Media tools to encourage effective customer interaction to better understand their sales and customer service requirements. A small business can better leverage social CRM if you can understand how best to apply it to your organization.

Essentially, Social CRM is about listening to customer conversations, analyzing those conversations, relating the acquired information to existing data with your company and taking action based on these customer conversations. CRM processes can seem quite intimidating. Businesses have to understand that CRM is all about the people. As a marketer, you have to understand that a brand is not what you tell your customers it is; rather it is what people say it is. The idea is that brands must avoid controlling the message and allow its customers to collaboratively shape its image. Training your employees to use Social Media networks like Twitter and Facebook to build relationships is the key. Be careful not to spam your customers and avoid advertising your products. Leverage Social Media networks to listen and engage your customers. Identify the right internal resources for customer service, marketing and sales and train them to prioritize Social Media conversations so that they do not get stymied by the sheer volume of conversations taking place in the Social Media space.

Sometimes, transparency can scare businesses, but to succeed in this age of consumer awareness, you have to experiment, take smart risks and learn quickly from every failure. The focus must be on sharing relevant information with your customers, empowering your sales and customer service teams to help customers and to provide immediate response, gathering feedback and enabling product teams to act on such feedback. A responsive customer service team must be a part of your corporate DNA. Offer customers with platforms like UserVoice or applications like Feedback on Facebook to provide direct product feedback and ensure that the feedback is heard and acted upon. Look at companies like Zappos and Comcast who have leveraged Twitter to connect with their customers and have built a loyal and interactive community based on customer conversations. Another important aspect is to consolidate and standardize all information gathered from customers across your locations. For example, when a customer makes an address change, be sure that it is reflected across all of that customer's records throughout the CRM application. This will ensure that the entire customer service organization is able to service them effectively and properly.

Identifying Your Social Customer
For companies, it is vital to understand social customers, their preferences and market behavior so that businesses can identify them and earn their trust. So who are the social customers?
- The social customer gets their breaking news through Facebook and Twitter and allows their views and opinions to be influenced by their Social Media peers;
- They learn about new products and brands through Social Media sites; instead of believing advertising rhetoric, they trust their Social Media 'friends' for honest feedback;
- They expect brands to be active on their social networks, to listen to their feedback and to engage with them; they expect brands to respond immediately to their queries and complaints or else, they are quick to move on to a competitor;
- Social customers are also quick to discuss their disappointments or unhappiness with brands on Social Media channels;
- They do not take kindly to unsolicited spam on their social networks but do not mind receiving relevant information.

**Leveraging value from existing customers**
It costs more to gain a new customer than to retain an existing one. In fact, Emmett C. Murphy and Mark A. Murphy say that the costs of acquiring a new customer can actually be five times greater than retaining existing ones. Businesses can increase their revenues more efficiently by leveraging existing customers.

One way is to increase the value of an average order. This can be achieved by upsells, cross-selling, suggesting recommendations and offering bundled products and services.
- An upsell is when a customer is convinced to buy a product which is better or has more features than the one he/she was considering to purchase. An upsell is more of a substitution. For example, if a customer is purchasing a new laptop from Dell, they get Microsoft Office for free or they can upgrade to the Professional version for an additional fee.
- Cross-selling involves convincing the customer to purchase additional products that complement or enhance the product they are already considering to buy. For

example, if a customer is considering the purchase of a Dell laptop, they can be offered a printer. So cross-selling is an addition to the order.
- If you have a record of what your customers have browsed or purchased in the past, you can recommend products that can appeal to them. Companies can also utilize data like location, gender and age to suggest recommendations to browsing customers. For example, if there is a record showing that people from New York browsing for a Mac also browse for watches and running shoes; you can recommend these products to your next customer from the city. Amazon is a great example of this method; they often recommend additional products under the heading "Frequently Bought Together."
- Another great way to entice your customers is to offer products in bulk (i.e. volume pricing) where the price of a single product decreases depending on the quantity ordered. So if you are selling perfume for $25.99, you can offer a 3-pack for $22.99 each (a total of $68.97). While your profit on a product unit has decreased, you have made it up in volume. You must highlight the discount in each case.

The other method is to increase the order frequency through the existing customers. So if your average repeat customer buys six times a year, you can aim to increase it to once every month – thus, doubling the value of that customer. So how can you make your existing customers keep coming back?
- A look at Zappo.com's success story tells us about the importance of meeting customer expectations, and at times, even exceeding them. Businesses can do this by providing high quality products, meeting delivery demands on time and always communicating with customers openly and honestly.
- Provide special treatment for your more valuable customers. Developing a communication channel helps build relationships with your customers. Status emails, a handwritten note with the shipment or a discount coupon for their next order are very personal ways in which customers can be made to feel special and inspire loyalty in them. This also helps you to maintain regular contact and offer targeted specials.
- If you are selling products that customers purchase more than once, offer them a reorder option. This can be a separate page that shows previous purchases by the customer and an "Add to Cart" button at the bottom of the page.
- Use the sign up form on your website or a mailing list application on Facebook fan pages to collect the emails generated to create a mailing list. You can then use this list to send details of new products, sales and gift ideas.

Remember, your customer is your best asset. Customers help your business grow, so make extra efforts to meet their needs. A satisfied customer will make additional purchases, and a customer who has been made to feel special will be loyal to you and will share his/her experiences with friends – that's free marketing for you!

**Dealing with unprofitable customers in efficient and cost-effective ways**
TXU, a large power provider in Texas, in 2005 implemented a tough marketing policy to deal with the pressure of a deregulated energy market. The company stopped services to late-paying customers and then charged them expensive reconnect fees, while offering perks to those who paid on time. This helped the company to reduce "bad debt" from non-paying customers as well as provided it with increased productivity from employees who were spending much time in fielding calls from this non-profitable segment. The company puts it this way: "A customer who calls you every day is less profitable than one who pays on time and never calls you."

In mid-2007, wireless service provider Sprint Nextel sent letters dismissing about 1,000 customers. The action followed a year of tracking a group of high-maintenance end users and the number and frequency of support calls made by them. The company found that these customers were calling customer care multiple times a month and were often found complaining about the same issues. The company concluded that it was unable to meet the billing and service needs of this tiny group and, so, cut off their service after waiving their termination fees.

So why do companies pull the plug on some customers? A major reason is the declining profitability of certain segments of customers and falling productivity of employees who mostly deal with such unprofitable customers. Some other reasons could be the company's changing business strategy and its struggles to serve large volumes of customers. There are collateral damages to divesting customers. Companies can get a reputation as a 'difficult' company and even retained customers may worry about being next in line and migrate to rival providers. To avoid it, instead of dropping customers immediately, companies can engage in reassessing the values of each customer and educating unprofitable customers, in order to reevaluate the importance of such customers. Divestment should be seen as a final decision.

But how do you identify unprofitable customers or calculate customer profitability? Most of the time, businesses do not like to admit that they have unprofitable customers. Are you spending more than expected on customers who do not provide equivalent returns? A simple way to find out is to breakdown revenue by customers, assuming that the cost of the products and service is the same for all customers. Companies also rely on signals like late payments, too many customer service calls and frequent complaints.

Let's discuss some key steps that experts and analysts advocate before businesses make that final call to terminate the relationship with a customer.

**Reevaluate the relationship with your customers:** Customers suggest that sometimes lack of information about your services, the changed needs of your customers, or the changed focus of your business, has led you to ignore certain customers.

**Inform and educate customers:** Provide information or training to 'problem' customers so that they understand your offerings better – this will ensure they have fewer questions and will take up less of your employees' time. Such customers can be taught to use automated phone lines (if you have them) or the company website for trouble shooting.

**Change your policies:** Consumer goods giant Procter & Gamble realized that direct LTL (less-than-load) shipments were raising costs. So the company changed its policy to ship goods in truckload volumes only. Consequently, smaller, less-profitable customers had to turn to distributors. Thus, P&G was able to differentiate its services to larger, more profitable customers.

**Stick to your strengths:** If your customers are asking for a service that you do not provide or are not skilled at, refuse them or even better, contract it to a specialist.

You can consider placing unprofitable customers under a new pricing structure in which they can be charged for extra services to restore the balance between the costs of service and benefits. You can also consider a different payment structure, for example, a prepaid service option. Or you can transfer them to a different channel or partner companies who may be better able to satisfy their needs. Give every customer a chance at being profitable.

Even after all efforts, if the 'problem' persists, you can drop the customer. Companies drop unprofitable products all the time, so why not customers? But do so gracefully, in a polite manner and in person so that your brand does not suffer from negative publicity. Always inform them in advance of your decision, particularly if a contract renewal date is looming close, and explain your reasons for the decision. Avoid sending emails and letters.

Finally, find out the characteristics of unprofitable customers. Also check if your marketing campaigns are targeting the right customers. If not, change your marketing and PR strategies. Find out what makes your profitable customers different from the unprofitable ones. Make sure that new marketing campaigns target people similar to your profitable customers. Brad Skelton, managing director of Skelton Tomkinson, who turned his company around by concentrating on profitable customers, said "I run my company with this saying: Volume is vanity, and profit is sanity."

## Recommended CRM Tools

### CoTweet

CoTweet can be used as both a CRM and marketing tool. CoTweet is a great tool that can enable small businesses to create a customer service approach to their engagement with consumers and train employees to share Social Media duties. CoTweet has been specifically designed to help businesses maximize their Twitter ROI. It allows businesses to manage multiple accounts and allows multiple users to access a single account. The CoTweet dashboard is similar to standard email inboxes. Businesses can set up custom search panels, view replies and direct messages, and select an individual handling a Twitter account for a view of their conversations, and make notes to share with team members.

CoTweet also enables businesses to assign roles so that certain team members are responsible for managing Social Media at certain times. Its On-Duty feature helps users specify if they are on-duty or off so that other team members can access the list and view the on-duty Twitter assignments. On-duty team members will also get email alerts whenever they receive a reply or a direct message to the Twitter accounts. Team members can also view Twitter activity across multiple accounts, so that duplicate actions are avoided. CoTweet allows you to monitor keywords and trends and helps you select updates and follow-up messages that can be assigned to specific team members. This allows for members with specific knowledge to handle the relevant questions and comments. CoTweet allows responders to add initials at the end of the tweet so that users and followers know that the responses are from a real person.

The standard edition service is free and allows up to six Twitter accounts but organizations can also avail of its enterprise option at a fixed fee per month. You can also request a free demo before you make a final decision to purchase. CoTweet supports Twitter and Facebook and recently launched an iPhone application. A number of big brands, including Ford, Pepsi, Best Buy, JetBlue and Microsoft, are already using CoTweet as a Twitter CRM tool.

### Salesforce

Enterprise cloud computing company Salesforce.com has introduced several different solutions under its platforms like Service Cloud and Sales Cloud, to help integrate Social Media with Salesforce. Some of these solutions include Salesforce for Twitter which lets you pull in and monitor Twitter feeds and accounts within the Salesforce.com CRM as well as Chatter, a Facebook-like solution for business. Salesforce for Twitter enables you to assign cases or leads based on a tweet which can be directly followed-up or monitored with other aspects of the work flow.

Chatter is a social platform for business communications, which boasts of features like 'groups' that allow businesses to create public and private groups. This enables them to share documents and status updates, address customer service concerns and communicate about projects. Then there is Jigsaw for Salesforce that integrates the Salesforce CRM and Chatter experience with Jigsaw's crowdsourced business data service. Jigsaw allows users to update and verify contact information, and share it with everyone in the Jigsaw network. Jigsaw also pushes out data about your contacts and leads through Chatter. The application also has charts and analytics that showcase the amount of money generated by each lead.

**Case Studies**

Counter Culture Coffee
North Carolina-based Counter Culture Coffee, which sells coffee to individual consumers, cafes, restaurants, and retailers across the country, sought a CRM platform that could help it expand its business and find additional markets for its products. At that point, the company was managing its accounts and customer support on its in-house database as well as on paper. It used a leading CRM platform, Salesforce, to automatically transfer service and product requests that arrived through the website to the appropriate salesperson. The company utilized Salesforce's various solutions like Sales Cloud, Service Cloud, Force.com and Chatter to streamline its business and service.

Sales Cloud enabled the company to build dashboards and reports to measure sales, marketing budgets, coffee information and blend changes; thus helping employees of various departments to work together efficiently. Service Cloud enabled the company to track all requests for service from the Web, email, and phone in Salesforce. The requests varied from inquiries about particular varieties of coffee to questions about equipment, in-store demos, marketing support, and tastings. The Cloud also integrated Salesforce with Gmail and Google Apps. The Force.com application helped build custom applications like Training Centers, which helped manage the logistics of the many events that Counter Culture holds around tastings, trainings, and other special events. The product development app

Producers, Lots, and Coffees maintains up-to-date information about producers so that an employee can link fresh or roasted coffee beans to a specific farmer anywhere in the world. It also built automated assignment rules to assign sample requests to the right people.

Members of the management, sales, customer support, and roasting departments also channeled Chatter to replace their weekly status report emails with Chatter status updates and feeds in a bid to communicate effectively. Chatter also enabled automatic broadcasts of associated activities allowing employees to stay tuned to the happenings regarding particular customers, training centers and products. The efforts resulted in increased efficiency in communication and customer data, and fostered a sense of community among employees who could see their colleagues' activities and could engage in conversations online. It also helped create a company culture as employees were now more knowledgeable about the activities of departments other than their own ranging from coffee to equipment sales to trainings to attendees at tastings.

### 24 Hour Fitness
24 Hour Fitness, one of the world's largest fitness chains, adopted Salesforce and various applications from its AppExchange marketplace to unify all its corporate sales groups on one CRM platform and get a consolidated view of its customers. The Pollzter for AppExchange helped the company to easily create and distribute surveys and response forms; the Sxip Audit helped in monitoring security status and updates and Mass Update Anything enabled bulk updating of any field on various records. According to the company, its Corporate Sales Department saw business grow 30% yearly. Apart from revenue growth, the company also witnesses better transparency, reporting, and communication across global teams.

### MAS Wine
Hopland, California-based MAS Wine, founded in 2006, uses its beer distributors to sell its products to restaurants, hotels, bars, and clubs. As the economic crisis deepened in 2008, the company wanted a CRM solution to track customer data, to increase sales and to control costs. The company decided to select Salesforce's Sales Cloud for its mass email functionality. The platform helped the company to record every business action in Salesforce, including phone calls, emails, and other tasks. It tracked the products shipped from the warehouse and sold to each customer, thus helping distributors to optimize orders and manage inventory cycles. The platform also helped the sales teams to build new customer leads. The CRM platform enabled the company's small team to achieve visibility across the business, close more deals, retain more customers and helped them maximize

achievements with fewer employees. Instead of distributors, the company also relied on the CRM platform to identify a number of prequalified buyers for their products.

**In conclusion:**
Existing customers are always more profitable than new customers. Eighty percent of your profits will come from 20% of your customers. Acquiring new customers costs businesses money and they probably tend to buy small.

On the other hand, it costs businesses less to service existing customers as you would most likely know and understand their requirements. Focusing your marketing efforts on current customers can offer you lower costs for additional sales, greater customer loyalty, higher customer satisfaction scores, and more profits. Also, they trust you and are hence, liable not only to purchase more often but also to buy the more expensive products and services. Most importantly, they will evangelize your brand among friends.

Word of mouth is the most powerful form of promotion. So engaging both existing and new customers on Social Media sites like Facebook and Twitter can enable you to interact with them and build a mutually beneficial relationship with them. Social Media sites also offer your customers easy platforms to share their experiences about using your products or services with friends. Businesses can use Social Media to promote their products and special offers, to address complaints and to communicate with their customers.

**In the next chapter:**
You will be introduced to online reputation management and monitoring and how Social Media has changed the game. We will discuss tips to select keywords and other tools to monitor reputation. We will also talk about strategies for reputation management. We shall also look at the popular Social Media sites than can help you monitor your online presence.

# Chapter 4

# Seven Deadly Sins of Social Media

# Seven Deadly Sins of Social Media Marketing

Worldwide Web users greatly dismayed by Petroleum giant BP's oil leak in the Gulf of Mexico took to Facebook and Twitter to express their outrage. Aggrieved online communities hotly debating the oil spill resorted to sarcastic comments like "Oil Oil everywhere, not a drop to use!;" "Texas tea time, wait till you see the crumpet;" and "We have put more birds in oil than Colonel Sanders."

This corporate crisis is a stark example of the evolving landscape of intense customer interaction and involvement in social, cultural, and economic issues that may or may not concern their day-to-day lives. Wal-Mart founder Sam Walton rightly stated: "There is only one boss; the customer, who can fire everybody from the chairman on, simply by spending his money somewhere else." Ironically enough, it was speculated that Wal-Mart's local Chicago public relations firm was behind a fake community support group that released blogs in support of the store coming to town. This was not the first time that the chain had been in the eye of a Social Media storm. In 2006, its PR firm rolled out a blog called Wal-Marting Across America, supposedly a chronicle of a couple's adventurous tour in an RV. Incidentally, the couple turned out to be one hired by the company itself.

Keeping aside the irony, the message here is that today's all-pervasive Social Media platforms have emerged as the most potent medium of public interaction. Both big and small brands, keen to appease the BOSS, are trying to leverage reach and power. However, in their anxiety to connect with audiences and drive new sales, businesses may end up making some silly mistakes, inadvertently. Like many of the big brands have already discovered, such goof-ups can permanently dent the brand image and business credibility.

The point is: Even while getting overawed by its enormous power, underestimating the nuisance value of Social Media can be a recipe for disaster. Thankfully, smaller businesses can learn from the costly mistakes made by their bigger counterparts. Here are the Seven Sins thou shalt shun to avoid embarrassment on Social Media.

### Sin 1: Being unfamiliar with Social Media etiquette
The networking sites are a social medium and hence, operate on the basis of personal identity. Social media interaction is similar to a face-to-face conversation and has its own norms. Recognizing the importance of polite behavior is important, as it can affect how companies are viewed and received by the online community.

We've already referred to the backlash faced by BP on Social Media. For example, Boycott BP, an enraged Facebook group, amassed well over 250,000 fans. Several US government agencies put up pages on YouTube, Facebook, and Twitter to tackle queries on the cleanup effort toward clearing the oil spill mess. And what was the company's official response? A spokesperson for London-based BP, Sheila Williams, simply stated that they were monitoring (negative) sentiment on Social Media sites, though online outreach was for them a lower priority than actually containing the spill. "Our view is that people are entitled to their views," she remarked. Of course, with the disaster still unfolding and its consequences expected to be felt for years to come, BP's reaction can be perceived in another way. Considering the extent of public outrage and media criticism, BP probably decided the best response was to keep a low profile and instead try to fix the problem as quickly as possible.

Now, here is an example of a company overtly disregarding public opinion! In March 2010, Greenpeace released a graphic online video, which admonished Nestle as one of the offenders of rainforest degradation. The company's Facebook page erupted in a flame war when the pro-environment organization protested the chocolate maker's alleged usage of palm oil from Indonesia's deforested areas. The Facebook page was flooded with queries seeking an explanation. Caught off guard, the company chose to respond in a rather unapologetic manner: "Thanks for the lesson in manners. Consider yourself embraced. But it's our page, we set the rules." Initially upset about the video, the users got further infuriated when Nestle apparently violated the implicit Social Media behavior norms. Most communications experts felt that the official posts put up in response to angry comments were overly flippant and excessively defensive giving fuel to the firestorm.

**Lesson to be learned: Thou shalt follow Social Media etiquette by proactively engaging users and practicing transparency, authenticity, and sincerity of communication**
At one level, Social Media denotes a form of publishing in which interesting stories get swapped and the exchange takes place within a community or a group. At another level, it denotes a way in which small businesses and publishers can pass their messages to their target audiences and prompt them to build strong connections and thus seek enhanced loyalty. Whichever way it's perceived, Social Media is now incredibly popular.

A McKinsey report states that two-thirds of all purchasing decisions are influenced by word of mouth mostly taking place on the Web. People trust friend opinions more than advertisements. Social Networking platforms definitely help smaller businesses identify new trends, build relationships and facilitate interaction with key contacts in the industry. But they can be equally hurting, if used recklessly. It is absolutely necessary to follow certain norms of user interaction while accessing them.

So here are the lessons to be learned:
- Determine the personality and identity of the brand and then match it to the individuals who will represent it online. As in customer service, your Social Media representatives must be trained to reactively and proactively respond to all critical things, which can affect brand perception.
- The three essential ingredients of a successful Social Media interaction are honesty, transparency and authenticity. Don't put someone in charge, unaware of the ramifications of flouting these norms.
- Engagement, not control, is a key ingredient to success on Social Media sites that facilitate one-on-one interaction and the rules of engagement here are quite the same as any face-to-face interaction. Never make the mistake of thinking that you can hold sway over conversations.
- Talk to your Social Media users like you would do in a real-life situation. In other words, stay away from overly composed or formal language. However, be respectful to users or else you will end up paying a heavy price in terms of a poor reputation for your brand. Reply to comments in an appropriate manner. Even while disagreeing with customer opinions, be polite.
- Avoid spam and off-topic or offensive remarks. Post meaningful content. What you share, tweet or post should reinforce your brand. Think and carefully construct each message. Provide unique perspectives on your business and products.
- Don't just talk or listen! Also try to act on the suggestions from users. Make it a point to learn from each engagement to improve your products and services.

## Sin 2: Treating Social Media as conventional Public Relations

Smaller businesses invariably feel the need to discover various cost-effective ways for addressing their consumers without compromising on brand integrity. Earlier, any PR activity was just about sending an invitation card, fax or e-mail. However, new innovative methods of distributing the information have emerged thanks to Social Networking channels. Even journalists and media personalities widely employ services like NewsBasis, and PRNewswire's ProfNet. Creating a custom landing page, communicating through Twitter with a BUDurl link to the press release, or perhaps directing to a YouTube video with the relevant announcement are some of the innovations being tried.

With the advent of Social Media, there has been a paradigm shift in both consumer interactions and the mode of addressing them. For example, customers today like to listen to clear-cut messages and frank comments from the company's top managers via blogs or tweets. This allows them to identify with the brand. Businesses need to grasp this significant transition and avoid treating Social Media as conventional Public Relations.

Here's how the chief executive of Wistia.com, Chris Savage, uses Social Media to build bridges with new clients. Randomly searching for phrases like 'private video sharing' on the networking sites, he comes across a post like this: "A teacher requested a private 'video sharing' site so that specialists can observe student behavior - can anyone refer one?" In this case, he instantly e-mailed and back came the reply: "YES! It's the first request for one - thought I'd hit up my tweets before (I) go digging." The CEO answered back: "Cool. You may want to check out Wistia.com. Full disclosure, I'm the CEO; -)" The firm in Lexington, Massachusetts that makes software for video sharing via a private network has greatly benefited from such smart Social Media usage.

Another example is that of Procter & Gamble's recent Social Media blitz, the response to which has been terrific. In no time, the Old Spice YouTube channel has recorded over 75 million total upload views. Is it possible to replicate a similar success with any conventional PR campaign? The answer is a big NO. It essentially carries a formal tone and approach. On the other hand, using Social Networking platforms in an innovative manner can greatly boost the brand presence thanks to their instant appeal and connectivity with the target audience.

**Lesson to be learned: Thou shalt grasp the differences between traditional PR and Social Media Marketing to fine-tune your strategy**
Social Media Marketing must be treated differently from traditional PR strategies. It is vital to grasp the nuances of an elaborate branding and marketing exercise on today's user-driven Social Networking platforms as compared to more conventional PR techniques. Here is a perfect practical example that illustrates the fundamental difference between traditional PR and Social Media marketing. A notice served by Federal regulators compels those who stand to make monetary gains from the review they are writing to be upfront about it.

The Federal Trade Commission (FTC) reported that a California marketing firm settled charges on its being engaged in false advertising. The firm had prompted its writers to host positive reviews of clients' games as part of the Apple iTunes Store. The reviewers gave these games excellent ratings with comments such as "One of the best apps just got better" and "Amazing new game." However, they failed to reveal the fact that they were compensated to do so. These charges were, in fact, the first ever to be framed under new guidelines set for Internet endorsements. Often deemed rules for bloggers, the guidelines also encompass anyone posting online reviews or promoting products/services through Twitter and Facebook. The attorney general in an official statement noted the action taken was to "strike against the growing practice of 'astroturfing,' in which employees pose as independent consumers to post positive reviews and commentary to sites and Internet message boards about their own company."

Such deceptive tactics tend to make prospective consumers wary of PR firms. Reacting to the case, an angry reader stated in The New York Times: *"What's funny about this incident is how inept 99% of PR firms are. This kind of nonsense from 'communications professionals' is rather common, and for each successful PR conceit, there're about a million, which are either self-defeating or deceptive."*

In another controversial case, Yelp has become the subject of public scrutiny after being made to face three class-action lawsuits from angered businesses. The owners claim that Yelp salespeople tried to press them into advertising by opting to manipulate reviews. Curiously, the site's motto is Real People. Real reviews! Its chief executive and co-founder Jeremy Stoppelman has vehemently denied the charges, asserting that the way the company works is counterintuitive to a lot of folks, which actually is the source of the whole problem.

A Yelp representative termed the allegations demonstrably false, since several businesses advertising on it have both positive and negative reviews, realizing that this gives value and authenticity to the entire exercise. In fact, there have been cases in the past of Yelp purging countless accounts after discovering that several businesses swapped goody-goody reviews with other owners. Many accounts and reviews simply disappeared from the site.

The series of events goes to underline the intricacy of Social Media marketing that makes it vastly different from conventional Public Relations.

So here are the lessons to be learned:
- Smaller businesses must use Facebook and Twitter to let prospective customers participate in the promotional effort. These channels also allow giving up some control to users, whereas traditional PR is mostly one-way. A typical PR plan will consume your precious resources to plan and execute it, whereas Social Media Marketing is dynamic, result oriented and most importantly, an ultimate no-cost way of marketing.

- Sticking to conventional PR and communication tools can prove to be a big drain on your business resources as they gobble up precious time, money and energy that small businesses can ill-afford to waste. On the other hand, Social Media can engage customers in a way that encourages trust and increases message retention. It's the new client relationship builder, thus turning the conventional PR strategies upside down.
- PR is no more a one-size-fits-all solution for every media and channel. It must reflect the shift to unique personalized consumption from mass consumption of information. Interactions have become more concise and focused, as brands are now in direct and constant contact with consumers via online channels. In the backdrop of this fast-evolving, consumer-centric communications landscape, it is not advisable to stick to a conventional PR approach, as you would be missing out on a larger audience hooked to Social Media. Most importantly, marketing and PR tend to work on a short-term basis and are mostly wedded to individual campaigns for meeting a short-term objective. Social media is not a temporary campaign. Rather, it's a permanent approach!
- Cross-platform PR campaigns that focus more on new media can deliver better results than one-dimensional marketing efforts. Take the case of brands like Sara Lee Deli and Land O'Frost, both selling sliced-meat products that prefer campaigns centered on Social Media rather than following a traditional PR strategy to reach current and potential customers.

**Sin 3: Not listening to the community but rather treating Social Media as a one-way megaphone**

Maintaining the brand's image in the public domain is a perennial and persistent challenge with which smaller businesses often find difficult to cope even with today's myriad media options. They need to understand that a meaningful Social Media presence can translate into brand awareness, user loyalty and importantly, increased sales. One of Twitter's co-founders, BIZ STONE, uses a peculiar term 'social alchemy' to denote the way in which seemingly inconsequential and innocuous messages can often get transformed into something of real business value. However, inexperienced players consider it as a channel only to brazenly promote their brand. They treat it as a tool to relentlessly evangelize about their products or services, showing little inclination to initiate conversations. This is a mistake because audiences are no longer interested in traditional message-oriented advertising.

Online media offers audiences the option to be selective of messages to watch/listen/read. They are more likely to associate with companies that engage with them. Take the example of Swedish company Elekta, which specializes in clinical oncology solutions. Almost invisible on the Internet, it took a series of steps like building a blog to provide useful industry-specific news, updates and information as well as directly communicating with customers. The strategy paid rich dividends.

**Lesson to be learned: Thou shalt not indulge in a one-way dialogue and shalt look to initiate genuine conversations**
You must not commit the mistake of treating Social Media as a one-way megaphone. It is also important to listen to the community. Social Media Marketing enables companies to build an engaged and active audience base and allows them to receive direct feedback from users. An honest response to it will convey to your customers an impression that you are genuinely interested in hearing them out. Coffee giant Starbucks is a great example. It has used social media platforms like Facebook and Twitter to engage with its base of over 7 million fans.

The company offers downloadable vouchers for free food or music with purchases. Its forum MyStarbucksIdea.com allows customers to make suggestions, to ask questions and to receive information about the brand. According to the company, it has implemented about 70 user-provided ideas. Such campaigns engage the online community and help improve the brand positioning.

So here are the lessons to be learned:
- Use the different Social Media channels to offer information through and about interesting articles, insightful blog posts and useful online services. If you are not doing that, you are only delivering a monologue.
- The key here is to listen and initiate conversations. Remember, Social Media is not a place to generate a monotonous monologue about your business. Conversation is a two-way street and any good conversation must have multiple participants.
- Blatant buy-buy messages will just not work. The best social media practitioners use the platform less for selling and more for interacting and engaging with potential customers. Listen carefully to what fans and even critics are talking about, both good and bad. This is a good practice as you may end up picking up excellent ideas for improving your business.

**Sin 4: Overstretching or using Social Media platforms without devoting proper time to them**
Social media is one of the hottest marketing trends at the moment. Companies - both big and small - are using online networks like Twitter to connect with their audiences and to promote their business. It is obviously tempting for them to seek spotlight on these popular channels. The online lending platform, Kiva.org, tried to increase the number of followers on its Twitter account by following the well-known

"#followfriday" concept. It turned out that #followfriday Twitter followers were the wrong audience for the campaign. Needless to say, the concept failed to click for the company.

Now let us see how the marine park SeaWorld used Social Media to create a buzz around its Manta Mania roller coaster ride in Orlando. It selected six influential bloggers and offered them exclusive access to the Manta site as well as SeaWorld. Their posts laid the groundwork for raising awareness about the park among tourists. Additional triggering posts, tweets and YouTube videos by visitors further increased awareness about the venue and its attractions.

**Lesson to be learned: Thou shalt be consistent and dynamic in Social Media conversations to hold the customers' interests**
Spreading yourself thin across the Web is not the way to a loyal brand following. After you have identified the right online network, devote enough time and energy to monitor the Web for mentions of the company, to comment on related blogs and also to contact online influencers.

A study by The Center for Client Retention, comprised of 22 Fortune 500 and Fortune 100 companies and including feedback from 27,000 consumers about their use and views of social media, found that 55% of consumers felt positively when companies responded to a social media post, with only 5% reacting negatively and 40% remaining neutral. So feedback, even negative in nature, is vital. Remember, in today's fast-paced digital world, negative content and comments can really spread like wildfire. Thankfully there are tools like search.twitter.com, TweetDeck and Twendz to track what Internet users are talking about you - be it in your backyard or across the globe.

So here are the lessons to be learned:
- Regularly update your Social Media profile to keep it dynamic and active by posting links to interesting articles and upcoming business events. Establish your Internet presence by launching a domain-specific blog.
- If someone does a search, you and your brand better show up in a bright light. With free-to-use tools like Yext Rep, you can avail of comprehensive Social Media and online reputation monitoring. You can check everything about your business or brand in the Yext Feed that allows you to monitor, and also respond to, reviews and comments on the Web.
- You also need to be savvy in your Social Media interactions because there are services like Rapleaf, a San Francisco based utility, which tracks the Web to compile specific status updates, the websites you link to, the comments posted

by you etc. The monitoring firm will gather all the relevant data and convert it into a 'social graph'. Some prospective vendors or partners may use this piece of information to dig deep into your Social Networks.
- Campaigns with a Social Media extension will keep coming and going, but what matters is maintaining an 'always on' approach and attitude. Your company's involvement in Social Media should not come with a deadline. It is essential that you sustain the Social Media interactions over a longer period to hold your customers' interests.

## Sin 5: Refusing to be transparent and genuine in your interactions on Social Media websites

Apart from being casual and irregular in your Social Media usage without devoting proper time to it, another cardinal sin is to be non-transparent in your approach. This is unethical in itself! Some businesses still commit the sin of deception, especially on review sites like TripAdvisor, posing as customers to create glowing reviews. Well, the strategy might work initially, but once users discover that your services or products fail to match the level of expectations raised, it is bound to backfire. Sometimes, Social Networking sites with their allure of minimal effort and immediate results can tempt businesses to go overboard or even indulge in false tricks, driven by an undue haste to promote their products or services. Look at what Honda did while promoting its Accord Crosstour on Facebook.

At the launch of the Crosstour model, the company posted its photographs on the Facebook page, ostensibly seeking comments and feedback. Unfortunately, the Facebook followers were not very impressed with what they saw. As negativity swarmed the site, Honda engineers lost patience. In an effort to counter the deluge of adverse publicity, they hosted a spate of positive remarks on their own. Incidentally, their identity was discovered, and embarrassed Honda officials had to undertake an extensive damage control exercise.

## Lesson to be learned: Thou shalt not be deceitful and dishonest in Social Media exchanges

Conversations on Social Media can be like walking on eggshells. Dishonest marketing techniques can never ever replace genuine customer-brand interactions. They can also lead to a loss of trust and business credibility. In case of any wrongdoing, Social Media spreads the negative word-of-mouth about the brand, product, or service. Hence you have to be very careful in ensuring that no deceitful and dishonest exchanges harm your business reputation. What then is the correct approach? Take the example of fashion blog Corporette. The popular women's business wear blog clearly indicated its affiliate marketing links so that readers were aware of revenue-generating clicks, and did not get misled.

So here are the lessons to be learned:
- If you hire a firm to handle your business promotions on Social Media sites and are part of any such association/affiliation, place a clear disclosure message on your site/blog.
- Effective Social Networking is about building meaningful, useful conversations and relationships with interested people. It's unimaginable that dishonest marketing techniques can ever score over genuine interactions.
- Remember, honesty is important to the trust-building exercise. Clearly indicate the affiliate marketing links on your blog so that readers are not misled about revenue-generating clicks.

**Sin 6: Paying people for customer reviews**
To beat the increasing online clutter, companies are turning to blog reviews to increase traffic to their sites, generate viral marketing and receive feedback on products. They resort to Social Networks with a large following or influential bloggers. Paid reviews are creative ways to place ad copy on the web in the form of actual unique content.

Take the case of Florida-based Joffrey's Coffee & Tea Company. To drive traffic to its site, increase branding in Social Media and promote the brand, the company invited over 1500 bloggers to try a free sample of 'Jamaican Me Crazy' flavored coffee. The campaign resulted in significant number of link backs to the beta site and the main business site. On the other hand, Alex Hunter tried to bribe the Top 10 Digg users to promote his website bringpopcorn.com. His message to them was: "Would you get my website to the Digg first page and if successful I'll pay $500". It was a wrong method to solicit to Social Media users.

**Lesson to be learned: Thou shalt be honest in using only genuine customer reviews about your brand**
John Chow, a prominent web marketing blogger, says "All I have to do is write at least 200 words and say it is a sponsored post, and then I can write anything I want—positive, negative or neutral."

So here are the lessons to be learned:
- If a business is of interest to the community, the company should promote it itself or hire a firm to handle Social Media promotions.
- Social Media's best practices demand that all disclosures must be clear and adequate. Such information must be easily visible to the customers.

- Bloggers should also disclose that they were offered free samples of the product and identify any sponsored links on their sites. This will inform customers that the review was not arranged by the company but was a credible assessment by the blogger. Such disclosures also help bloggers to protect their hard-earned reputation.

**Sin 7: Focusing on quantity of conversations you initiate instead of quality**
It is understandable that all competitive businesses aspire for an enhanced online presence via popular Social Media channels. But having an account in each and every sundry Social Network is not the correct approach to building a loyal brand community. Having hundreds of contacts across several networks may help you win a popularity contest, but it will not necessarily fetch increased sales and bigger profits.

There is an alternative to this mindless approach. Cynthia Drasler, founder of Phoenix-based chemical-free, personal-care products firm Organic Excellence, entered the realm of Social Media by taping an online weekly radio show in 2006. The weekly podcasts helped her build business credibility.

**Lesson to be learned: Thou shalt be selective and shalt only initiate quality conversations**
Spamming and frequent postings on Social Media sites can backfire by prompting users to leave your network. Thoughtful leadership is not sharing random links. Instead post regular articles, news updates and suggestions to build quality relationships. By simultaneously conversing with too many people, you risk the danger of going unheard amidst the din.

So here are the lessons to be learned:
- The focus should be more on connecting with people instead of garnering sheer numbers. Especially, smaller businesses must invest time in listening to a tight group of connections as this can bring in more profitability.
- Niche communities having an engaged discussion is more valuable than hundreds of people simply sharing links. Building these communities takes time, persistence and knowledge, and once in place, the rewards can be tremendous.
- Believing that promotion is all about regularly posting articles is a mistake. It's more about keeping the readers informed, providing them with news and helpful suggestions, and not simply spamming them with random links. Frequent postings with no real substance on Social Media sites can alienate users.

**In conclusion:**
It is imperative especially for budding businesses to integrate Social Media channels into their communications strategy. Social Media can be effectively used to enhance brand proposition. And here is how:

1. A flurry of innovations has reshaped consumer relations and the interactions landscape. A mix of social and mobile channels has enabled real innovation in conventional public relations building exercises, driven by technological advances. They offer a two-way communication platform for companies to tap user conversations.
2. There is a clear shift towards the trend of the 'social media release'. A host of services such as PressLift, PitchEngine, MindTouch and PRX Builder have transformed the ubiquitous press release with embedded multimedia features and easy distribution via various networking channels.
3. Know precisely what you want to achieve while conceptualizing a Social Media strategy. Ask whether you wish to generate more customers for your products and services, or you want to build a positive brand image. Be clear and specific about your goals. Accordingly, put in place a realistic plan with an emphasis on industry-specific niche Social Media sites.
4. Remember, it's the PEOPLE, who set the rules on Social Media, and those violating 'the will of the majority' will face inevitable consequences. The omnipresent networks make it easy to spread around any negative word, so don't alienate your followers and even your opponents.
5. You need not camouflage facts. Customers will appreciate knowing that the reviews are credible assessments not paid copy. Conversely, dishonest communication will erode trust. Keep your dialogue simple, honest and straightforward to initiate a customer-centric conversation.
6. Social Media interaction is not simply about marketing or merely about direct selling. Do not project yourself as an Internet marketer. Instead, try to see what your customers want and try to meet their needs.
7. Even the most promising and highly customer-driven businesses are prone to make mistakes since they are still in a nascent stage of Social Media Marketing. This is understandable, but the key is to admit the mistakes and to learn from them.
8. Use Social Media to become a thought leader or an idea generator in your niche space. This will automatically drive new customers to your business.

If you keep in mind these basic things, you are sure to be on your way to creating and building lasting relationships. Ideally, approach a reliable resource to help your company navigate the tricky emerging media waters, or else it may well imperil the 'social voice' of your brand. At the end of the day, every budding business must strive to earn its well-deserved social currency. Remember, there are no substitutes or shortcuts to genuine engagement and attachment in the realm of Social Media.

**In the next chapter:**
We will discuss and review blogging for small business sales success and the various strategies to make your blogs more effective.

# Chapter 5

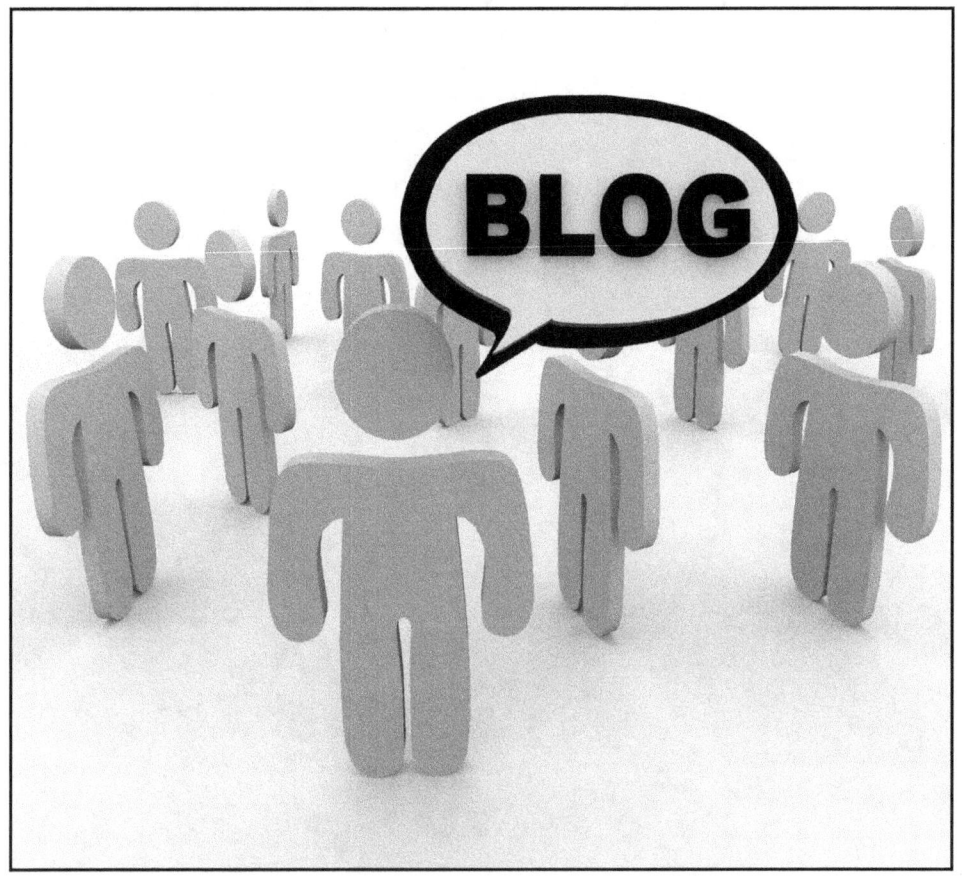

# Blogging for Small Business Success

## Blogging for Small Business Success

To understand why blogs are a critical part of your social media strategy, just scan through a report released by the world's leading market research firm, Nielsen, from June 2010:

- Consumers in the US are now spending more time on the Internet. The Nielsen report states that a significant chunk of time spent on the Internet is social in nature. Activities like messaging, commenting, sharing and blogging now take up more than 20 percent of the time spent by people online, each month.
- The users spend one in every four and a half minutes of their total time online on a social network or blog. In all, they spend 110 billion minutes on these interactive platforms, each month.
- The study notes that nearly three-quarters of consumers, who go online, visit blogs or social networks.

The data clearly points to the astonishing reach and influence of the widening blogosphere that budding businesses cannot simply afford to ignore. Now follow this real-life example to check the other side of the bright 'blog' story:

Absolut Vodka offered to sponsor Brooklyn Blogfest, an annual blog festival. A marketer representing the company offered gifts to bloggers for coverage. In no time, its 'favorable' mentions popped up on most blogs, with hardly any of them disclosing their 'relationship' that developed with the sponsor or mentioning the gifts given to them. And suddenly, they were faced with a marketing memo online! The unsavory controversy marred the festival and exposed the debatable ethical territory business blogs risk operating in.

So even though the promise of a business blog is in its unfiltered voice, the same can backfire, too! It's absolutely essential, as Absolut Vodka found out, to understand what exactly makes the platform all-pervading and powerful without trampling upon business ethics. How can you use the all-encompassing blogosphere to your advantage even while striking this fine balance? This is exactly what we shall find out!

Let us first define blogs before we consider their role in your marketing strategy. Blogs are essentially Internet journals to make regular entries on a particular subject. It's a combination of relevant text material with images and links to other blogs or news stories that elaborate on it. Wouldn't it be interesting to rewind the time clock to peer into the past of the blog? It evolved from the online diary earlier used to publish on personal websites or other online journals. Blogging was further popularized with the introduction of hosted blog tools like the Open Diary. Launched in 1998, this online diary community was probably the first to introduce reader comments. In 1999, Brad Fitzpatrick started LiveJournal. Launched in the same year was Blogger - later acquired by Google. In time, the evolution of advanced software has made it possible to host blogs on a variety of Web hosting services.

**Different types of blogs**
While blogs are primarily textual, there is also some focus on photographs, videos, music or audio. Their interactive format enables readers to leave comments. Let us follow the different types of blogs that can be used selectively to spread the word around, about your business.

**Personal blogs:** A sort of ongoing journal by an individual, it's the most common blog type. They are a combination of a diary, opinion posts and research links. Many people use them to generate income directly or drive traffic to other sites - for example, sethgodin.typepad.com

**Business blogs:** They help a company or organization to communicate with customers or employees and share their knowledge and expertise about the industry. Blogs can help businesses to generate traffic as well as connect with potential customers. For example, you can follow Jonathan Schwartz, CEO, Sun Microsystems, Inc. at blogs.sun.com/jonathan/

**Video blogs:** These are entries where you embed videos or video links along with supporting text and images in your blog. You can record videos in any of the popular formats like MP4 or WMV and serve through RSS feeds. You can even record live business in audio or video format to share it with the users. For example: videos.smallbusinessnewz.com/

**Photo blogs:** They are for sharing and publishing photos to communicate messages. They became popular in the 2000s with the advent of camera phones. For an example, see marktucker.wordpress.com

**Podcasts:** These comprise audio files available for download and playback on a personal computer or a mobile device like the iPod. Audio can be recorded in MP3 format and served through RSS feeds. You can use your mobile phone to write a blog post and even post pictures taken from your camera phone.

Most often, your blog may resemble multiple blog types, so the key is to organize its content such that you can categorize them easily.

**Popular blogging platforms**
If you are building a blog for your business interaction and enhancement purpose, you should substantially invest in it in terms of research and resources. Let's look at some of the most popular blogging platforms for the purpose.

**Blogger.com:** It's a free blog publishing platform formerly known as Pyra Labs before Google acquired it in 2003. Blogger has a very simple click, copy and paste interface. You can utilize the template-editing feature to customize templates. However, blogs cannot be customized to the extent as other providers. It is quick and simple to post pictures. Blogger's greatest advantage is its easy integration of Google's AdSense service. You can have group blogs on Blogger as well as restrict viewing access. Google Docs as well as Windows Live Writer have direct publishing integration to Blogger. Blogspot is not a search engine friendly format. Also, the blogs can be deleted at the blogger's discretion.

**WordPress.com:** This is another popular, free Weblog hosting provider since 2005. A favorite with professional bloggers, it offers a large variety of templates. You can customize your blog to make it look like a website. But you do not have easy access to the HTML code and posting pictures is slightly complicated. It allows you to cloak posts from selected users, and offers numerous plug-ins with greater versatility. Most of the features on the site are free, but a template editor and domain mapping will cost extra. You cannot host AdSense on a free WordPress blog, and you are restricted to one affiliate link per post.

**LiveJournal:** Commonly called LJ, it serves as a virtual community for users to keep a blog or journal. LJ allows multiple authors to post and it facilitates comments, calendars, and polls. With the 'friends list,' users can mark others as Friends to follow their journals and manage privacy settings. Templates can be customized as per requirement. If you are a paid user, you can add 'voice posts.' You may also simply call into the system and record an entry. It has integrated Google AdSense to enable paid users to generate revenue.

**Tumblr.com:** This mini-blogging platform allows users to post text, photo, video, links, and audio. It has a simple sign-up process and offers easy customization and use. You can install ready templates into your blog or make one of your own. The ability to customize a Tumblr blog is limited. It also does not have a built-in commenting system. You can add Google AdSense and Google Analytics into your

Tumblr blog. The best part is that you can create blog posts through email!

**Posterous.com:** Launched in 2009, it is designed more for mobile blogging. From your mobile, send an email with an attachment of text, images, video and audio files and the platform will create the post for you using this content. It boasts integrated and automatic posting to other social media tools like Flickr, Twitter, and Facebook; a built-in Google Analytics package and custom themes. Posterous has a built-in commenting system. Its URL shortening service allows users to post to Twitter. Being self-hosted, you need not worry about the platform deleting your blog.

**Strategies for successful blogging**
Blogs are a dime a dozen in these days of social media frenzy in literally every business domain. But only a select few of them are ultimately successful. So what are the strategies that can make for successful blogs on the Web? Here are a couple of pointers:

1. Successful blogging is about connecting with a target audience. You do not have to be a great writer or even be the most prolific. You just have to post relevant content on your blog.
2. Ensure the flow of dialogue and nurture your relationship with readers through comments and links.

We shall now discuss in depth some more critical strategies for successful blogging.

Create unique content
On the Web, unique and meaningful content is the stepping-stone to develop a standout blog. Aim at creating content that can bring value for your audience. It should be educational and informative in nature. Explore the Web for news and articles and provide your own perspective to them. A succinct synopsis will act as a quick key to grasp your ideas. Use humor, anecdotes, and first-person accounts so that your readers relate with the topic.

Comments build relationships
Blogging is about starting and maintaining a conversation. Monitoring comments ensures that conversations are kept going. You surely would not want to miss out on what people are talking about your brand. While replying to comments, be aware of the fact that your audience is keenly following you. Avoid sounding rude or aggressive. Provide further context to your comments in your responses so your readers can benefit from the ongoing conversation. Take the case of Kodak's blog,

A Thousand Words, which focuses on telling a story through photographs. With their gripping visual and textual content, the blog posts receive spontaneous comments. The writers make it a point to respond to them.

## Welcome constructive criticism

Always be prepared to receive even negative comments gracefully. Do not let any criticism about your ideas or actions upset you. Look at it as an opportunity to carry on conversations. The blogosphere appreciates a balanced response to constructive criticism, which can also help your product development process. Accepting criticism is extremely important to promote healthy interaction with your audience. A Washington Post article on Hardwood Artisans attracted negative comments for implying that the company did not provide health insurance for its employees. The company responded first by thanking the readers for their feedback, and later by explaining how it handled the particular issue. After the official response, more than 90 percent of the readers posted positive remarks and even defended the company.

## Track your conversations

Tracking conversations on your blog can help you keep track of the discussion in progress and also keep the dialog flowing. Most blogging platforms have notification technology, which can let you know in case of a new post or a new comment. Some blogs have comment email subscription available. You can also use tools like del.icio.us or yacktrack to track comments. Regularly monitor the Web for mentions of your company. Use RSS feed search engines like technorati.com and blogpulse.com to seek out corporate blog posts as well as important developments in your industry. The Google Alerts service is a great way to monitor any mentions of your posts.

## Talk about products selectively

Of course, you must utilize your blog to announce and discuss your products and services. However, avoid relentlessly hyping your products/services or promoting your brand on the blog. The audiences will not find it very appealing to listen to your business incessantly. People tend to associate more with companies that initiate and engage in conversations. Exploit the platform to promote your company as a resource of information and an expert on your industry. For example, Stonyfield Farm, a New Hampshire-based organic yogurt maker, discusses health and environmental issues, healthy living for women and kids, and shares tidbits about life on a farm through its blogs. The farm has built itself up as a brand based on positive responses to interesting posts like a call for environmental action.

## A few blogging blunders to avoid

For a small business, creating a blog may not always be easy. It takes a lot of hard work and creative ability to promote your brand and business. If not handled correctly, your blog strategy can backfire and make users lose interest in your business. This will not only fail to attract new customers but also turn away your existing customers. There are a few blunders that you must guard against. Let's discuss them here!

### Avoid irregular posting

Stick to a regular schedule so that your readers know when they can expect a new post. Put up quality content consistently so that they keep coming back for more information. Gradually, you can build your own loyal community. Involve more people in the task of managing the blog. It is better to avoid placing the burden of blog uploads on one single person.

### Do not wait to enable comments

The first thing to do once your blog is operational is to enable the comments section. Replying to comments can help build a community around your blog and will provide quality feedback. When your readers leave comments elsewhere on the blogosphere, your blog community will grow along with the cycle of quality feedback, thereby promoting your business. This will create awareness of your blog and bring in other readers. Blogging is a tool to connect with your customers – prospective and existing - so always encourage them to respond to your posts.

### Avoid treating your blog as a blatant PR tool

Your blog is not part of your public relations strategy. Blogging facilitates conversations with your customers. However, a self-promotional approach will turn them away. Instead, use it to share your insights about the industry, everyday life and processes at your company, as well as provide tips and information about the business.

### Do not get impatient

Do not expect social media to make your business an overnight success. Initially, it will seem as if no one is reading your blog, but do not get impatient or discouraged. Remember, it will take some time to build an enhanced community of readers. Brace yourself for the long run and continue posting unique content.

## Blogging and Search Engine Optimization

Ensure that your blog is visible online with the usage of the right search engine optimization (SEO) techniques. SEO is the process of improving both flow and quality of traffic to a website or blog from leading search engines through unpaid and algorithmic search results. This is not the same as other forms of search engine marketing (SEM), which may deal with paid search results. The higher a website appears in the search results list, the more visitors it will receive from the popular search engine. Blogs, by their very nature, attract search engine traffic. Most blogging platforms already have optimized site architecture. They have clear navigation with every page linking back to the other main pages. Let's study a few simple steps toward optimizing your blogs for search engines.

## Optimum usage of keywords

Keywords are specific terms or phrases that people use to search for information on search engines. Identify specific keywords for each post. Repeat them in the post just enough times to explain the theme. Use the keywords in your post titles, categories and page URL names. Do not overdo it such that your blog looks like a listless keyword catalog. The title must be short, succinct and catchy so that your readers can immediately recognize the crux of your post. Also, search engines use post titles to drive traffic to your blog.

## Regular and in-depth posts

Make it a point to post your blog entries regularly. This will make your blog look better to the search engines. Also, longer posts allow for more keywords that provide good search engine results. It can also contain more information. If you link correctly, your readers can be taken to different parts of your blog.

## Proper categorization of posts

Use categories to aggregate your blog entries according to the theme and topic. Each post can be placed in about 2 to 3 different categories based on its content. This will allow search engines to recognize your blog content and give it a chance of ranking well on these topics. Avoid overkill by adding too many general categories.

## Effective archiving methods

Carefully organize your blog archives into subjects and date ranges. You can either offer the entire content of every post in a category on the archive pages, or simply link to each post with a text snippet. Whether linking to one of your previous posts or to a post by another blogger, provide an anchor text. For example, instead of just writing 'Click here', you can say, "Seth Godin on what makes famous slogans." This is beneficial from the point of view of search engine rankings.

Identify forums active in your domain
Blogs attract more incoming links compared to websites. A great source of posts to social news and social media sites, they also allow for easy sharing of text, audio and video. Identify bloggers and forums that are already active in your industry. You can search for related communities using Technorati or Del.icio.us tags. Submit your blog to directories like Technorati. These are great resources to secure one-way links.

Watch your analytics
Enable visitor-tracking software like the free Google Analytics on your blog. Tracking software will tell you how the top search engines are delivering traffic. You can use this information to fine-tune your blogging strategy.

Content is king
Most importantly, focus on the right content in your blogs. Tackle topics that will elicit queries, doubts and suggestions from your customers. Write with passion and it will show in the blog output. Try to insert images, bullet points and graphs. Use videos and interactive elements like polls, to create appealing posts.

Marketing your blog successfully
With so many new blogs being created every day, optimizing your blog to ensure maximum online visibility may seem like an intimidating task. Let's consider some vital blog marketing and optimization tips.

Host your blog on your domain
It is best to host your blog on the same domain as your primary business website. This will attract links, attention, publicity, and better search rankings. Blogger and WordPress will allow you to use their hosted platform and display it on your own domain. Avoid hosted platforms that do not let you create your own domain name.

Choose the right blog software
Choose blog software that can be customized for your corporate blogging purposes. You can select blogging platforms like WordPress, which already have optimized site architecture. You could also create a blog from scratch for flexibility in terms of functionality and formatting. Ensure that features like comments, archives, sub-pages, categorization and multiple feeds are active. Most blogging software will offer fairly simple URL structure, thus making it easy for search engines to find blog content. Your blog layout, sidebars and links must convey the purpose and meaning of the content on your blog. Select appropriate colors, lines, photographs and illustrations to complement your message.

### Use links intelligently and selectively
Links within your blog posts must be part of the content. Every post does not need a link. Use your discretion while linking stories. However, if you are quoting or discussing other bloggers' ideas or online sources, it is good to link them. They will feel flattered and often will link back to your blog, sending some readers your way. Identify well-known blogs and websites for your blogroll – the more links you have on your page, the better you are likely to rank on search engines.

### Invite guest bloggers
You can invite a well-known personality in your industry to share their niche expertise with your audience. You can also invite other bloggers to present their unique perspective. Thus you will assure yourself a link or an association with a brand. However, do not edit guest posts without their consent.

### Provide a unique look at your niche
Write original content instead of rehashing someone else's story. Offer valuable and different content rather than the same run-of-the-mill story retold. If you are in an industry with a dense presence in the blogosphere, every major news or development is not worth mentioning unless as a shared experience into your blog.

### Share as much as possible
Sharing information like trade secrets, pricing, contract issues and an occasional rumor can benefit your blog. Take a call early on what you consider off-limits to be posted on the blog and then slowly push the limit to see the best results. Your efforts will be rewarded in the form of increased traffic. Register your blog with popular search engines like Google and Yahoo. Describe it in precise words. Mention your niche market and topic so that they can find you better.

### Add RSS to your blog
Many hosted platforms may not have RSS automatically available, but you can add it. People look for the orange RSS logo when they want to subscribe to a blog. So guarantee visibility by placing the RSS links in the sidebar of your blog. With FeedButton, you can offer multiple RSS aggregator buttons with a single expanding rollover button. For people uncomfortable with RSS, offer an option to get your blog posts by email. Tools like FeedBlitz make this service automatically available on your blog.

You can try out the tactics above to get a head start in the world of blogging. Let's review a few important aspects that hold the keys to successful marketing of your business through blogs:

1. Treat your readers and customers with respect. Offer them quality information and unique perspectives so that they are always keen to connect with you and your brand.
2. Request feedback and reviews of your blog.
3. If you have a post that can help others, point to it in relevant forums and discussion threads.
4. Contact other bloggers or sites and offer guest posts. Highlight quality content from other blogs and leave comments on relevant industry-related blogs and sites.
5. Try and help other bloggers so that they boost visibility of your blog in online and offline forums. Add the trackback feature to encourage interaction.
6. Interviews with other bloggers from your business domain can build interest and additional content for your blog as well as generate links and more traffic.
7. Last but not the least, focus on the right content in your blogs. Spend time and effort to research the subject before posting your views. You may hire a blog consultant to streamline your content to attract traffic.

Before we conclude, go through this interesting case study and decide for yourself how you want to approach blogging for business success.

An e-mailed invitation from LOFT (popularly known as Ann Taylor LOFT) was passed among fashion bloggers for an event in New York. It had an unusually pointed footnote. Many thought that the invite for an 'Exclusive Blogger Preview' of their Summer 2010 collection was inappropriate. Why?

"Come take a sneak peek at LOFT's collection before anyone else!" the flier stated. It promised a gift to every attendee and a guaranteed entry into a "mystery gift card drawing." However, the company got down to real business by stipulating: "All bloggers must post coverage from the event to their respective blog within 24 hours in order to be eligible. Links to it must be sent to the address (mentioned), along with the code on the back of a gift card given to you at the event. You'll be notified of your card amount." The rejoinder was mentioned in small print at the bottom. In response to the footnote, a company representative stated: "Engaging the blogging community is a new way for us to communicate product information." Is the company right in promoting its business in this manner? What's your take?

**In conclusion:**
There is a fine line between what is ethical and what is unethical in the world of blogging. Even as blogs take their deserving place alongside conventional media, businesses need to steer clear of regulations. In fact, the federal government has been issuing guidelines in an effort to step up enforcement, and make sure that a marketing campaign is properly disclosed.

It's indeed a crowded blogosphere but the strategies mentioned above should help you score over the competition. Just to sum up, the most important aspect of blogging, going beyond money making opportunities, is to build a brand that people want to associate with – and that too, in an ethical manner. Remember, a comprehensive blogging platform gives your customers an opportunity to establish a lasting association with your brand.

**In the next chapter:**
We shall discuss using Facebook and elaborate on ways to create an impressive profile and business page. The next chapter will highlight strategies to build a successful business through Facebook as well as examine case studies of businesses that saw a turnaround after connecting with their customer base through Facebook. We shall also study the impact an active Facebook page can have on customer relations and resulting profit margins.

# Chapter 6

# Facebook

# Facebook: The Mass Media of Our Time

Facebook, the most talked about social network of the new millennium, started off as a site only for Harvard students and employees, but in a short span of time, it grew to become the world's largest social network site.

Facebook has also emerged as a great marketing tool for small businesses. What makes the platform The Mass Media of our Time? This is exactly what we will try to find out!

Facebook allows users to add friends and send them messages, as well as update profile pages to notify friends about themselves. The friends have access to each other's pages, photos, videos, blog streams, and any other form of content posted by the user. Users can also join networks organized by workplace, school, or college.

Businesses find it convenient because it's free and fairly easy to navigate. If you are someone not conversant with social media, think of Facebook simply as a networking event that allows you to spread the word about your business. By investing requisite time, energy and effort, you can build a strong brand loyalty, effectively engage with your customers, prove your expertise and drive good traffic to your website.

A glance at the features
Facebook offers several cool features for users. Let's check some of them out:
1. You can post messages and share attachments on the Wall of your profile page.
2. You can tell your friends about where you are and what you are doing by updating your Status messages.
3. With Pokes, you can send a virtual 'poke' to a friend.
4. You can upload photo albums and videos for sharing with friends.
5. Facebook Notes allows you to import blogs from blogging services like Blogger.
6. When you join a Facebook group or users become fans of your page, Facebook adds a feed item to their Mini Feed automatically that can be viewed by everyone on their profile pages. The News Feed then combines each user's mini feed into a single news item, which appears on your homepage. This offers a good scope for your online marketing.

## The Fan Page - Build a platform for your business

Facebook profiles are for your personal account. If you are looking to create a Facebook presence for your business, create a Fan Page. Provide information about your company, upcoming events, share photos and videos, create discussion forums and add links back to your business site.

Pages have 'walls' where fans can post. 'Updates' are shown on the update tab as well as the walls of fans, if they have allowed the page to show updates. You can also add applications like an RSS (Really Simple Syndication) feed from your blog or embedded videos from YouTube to increase the functionality of your page. With these pages publicly available, search engines can easily find and index them.

The fan page is essentially your company's profile page. Use it to express your commitment to your brand, company, product or service. Weave credible and real experiences around your brand or product to convey their intrinsic values. A strong profile can be a great marketing tool, as it allows you to showcase your expertise, explain what your business can offer and also build your credibility. It can help you make connections with your peers and convert them into partners or customers. Your personal information, work information, photos and applications on the page must relate to your brand.

Remember, users respect authenticity and transparency. Make sure your brand is entwined with your personal identity. What you convey on this page will decide whether your friends connect with you, your identity and your business. Also, people do not want to be serious all the time so present things with a touch of humor! For example, Zippos posts crazy videos on their Facebook page.

You cannot add friends on Facebook pages like you can from your personal profile. People have to choose to become fans. So you have to keep introducing the page to as many users as possible. Promote your company page through emails, blog and through Facebook groups, to build up your network. Connect with as many customers, associates, and friends on Facebook so that you can drive targeted traffic to the fan page.

Avoid having any elements on the page that do not relate to your business. Look at it this way: Does your page have anything you would not like to see published in a newspaper? For example, personal details like beach pictures of your last vacation are inappropriate to share with business colleagues and clients, so avoid posting them.

**Facebook Groups – Connect with your network**
Facebook groups are viral marketing at its best! So seek out and join relevant networks and groups. They are basically communities of friends with similar interests. These are different from fan pages.

Small businesses can create Facebook groups to further brand promotion, share news/events with community members and encourage discussions. Offer vital information like contact details, website and location. Also, enable everyone to post discussions, pictures and videos. Invite friends, email contacts, blog readers and subscribers, among others, to join your group. Update the news, photos, videos, events and links regularly to give the group members a reason to return. You can also create a welcome message to greet new members.

**Fan Pages or Groups?**
Though pages and groups have many overlapping features, there are vital differences. What are they?
1. Facebook Groups, by nature of their security features and size limits, enable better personal interaction while Pages are used to represent corporate identities.
2. Significantly, Pages get indexed by search engines unlike Groups.
3. Groups are either closed or open. By default, they are closed. In this case, every new member to a Group must be approved by the Group's Administrator. However, access to a page can only be restricted by age and location. Pages can also be better customized compared to Groups.
4. Groups are great to organize intense interactions around a cause or any topic of general interest, whereas Pages are better for promotion of brands, businesses or products without any need to connect customers to a personal account.
5. You can add extra applications like Twitter, YouTube, Flickr on your page, whereas these cannot be added on groups.

**Marketing your business better via Facebook**
While companies are increasingly turning to social media to promote their business, they are also discovering that it's a challenging process. Small business owners must understand the fact that to build a successful social media presence, they have to be active, sincere, transparent and creative in their efforts. Importantly, they must avoid too much hard selling and promotion.

Facebook offers demographic features, which can help marketers target the advertisements to customers, depending on parameters including age, gender, location, and education. This allows you to easily target your niche audience base. Let's discuss some marketing strategies for small businesses to succeed on Facebook.

<u>Spread the word</u>
Once you have built a Fan page, you should begin promoting the page to increase

visibility of your brand. As you cannot add friends to this page, you must focus on introducing the Page to your friends, partners, associates, and employees, urging them to join and share the Page with their respective friends. This way, you can get more people to become fans as well as build your network.

Identify your niche audience
Seek out groups that host your prospective customers in larger numbers. Ensure that the groups are from your domain. Focus on processes or systems relevant to your own business. Identify the key people in these groups and send them friendship requests along with personal messages.

Track your fans' conversations
Spend some time tracking the topics that your Facebook fans are discussing. Take note of their status messages and the people with whom they connect. Study the subjects and types of messages that elicit the biggest response. Most importantly, identify topics that they tend to avoid.

Join the conversation
Identify the hour of the day (or the night) when most of your fans are active on Facebook. Accordingly update your Facebook page. For example, you can update your status earlier in the morning before starting work, at mid-day or late in the afternoon. Your messages should not always be business-related; they should fit in with the core conversation.

Up the service ante with Discussion Forums
If you do not have a service forum on your website, open a forum under Discussions on your company's Facebook page and let your customers know that they will receive service support there. Check the forum for issues every hour. This will provide your customers with a direct platform to get solutions for their specific problems.

Be consistent and proactive
Update your blog regularly and write articles based on conversation topics from Facebook. Send a message to your fans with a link of these articles. Always be on hand to congratulate your fans or celebrate any good news. Share the news with your fans. Avoid getting into arguments and stay neutral in case of one.

Run creative campaigns
Facebook members, who are popular, invariably receive a good amount of messages. For this to happen, your message has to be special enough to garner everyone's attention. Instead of shooting off uninspiring messages, think differently

to draw users to your page. Why not leave a message on your Facebook page informing all members that you will be on Twitter at a certain hour when they are welcome to communicate with you. Or how about this: Hold a contest and give out prizes. For example, a user who becomes the 50th or 100th subscriber to your blog will get an incentive or run a simple contest for fans to participate in a fun video or photo challenge.

Facebook ad platform
Facebook's advertisement platform is considered one of the most effective ways to access your target audience. Facebook ads have the advantage of filtering through users' profile pages for their age, location, interests and other information that helps in the process.

Let's now take a look at some small businesses and entrepreneurs who have tasted success with the help of Facebook.

**These big players made a connection**
In this section, we will consider some highly successful Facebook campaigns.

Adobe plays Facebook
Software maker Adobe wanted to raise awareness of its discounts for college students. So the company created a Facebook campaign around a game that asked Fans of the Adobe Students which of the series of images was 'Real or fake?' The answer screens for the Photoshopped images included a tutorial that showed users how each effect was achieved using Adobe's product. At the end of the game, there was a promotion for Adobe Creative Suite 4 Student Editions and call-for-action buttons like Buy Now, Play Again and Share with friends.

The company also placed visible messaging asking users to return by informing that five new images would be posted each week. The Fan Page also had a discussion board, which encouraged users to share their scores and talk about the game. During the month long campaign, the game was played over 14,000 times, 6% of the users clicked the "Buy Now" button at the end of the game, and the Page received over 50,000 clicks with the addition of over 5,000 fans. Even before the campaign was launched, the Adobe Students Page had featured the student pricing message, but lack of engagement kept the target audience away. A fun and engaging feature brought the audience to the page and generated awareness of its offer as well as the value of the product.

## IKEA's inspired move
Furniture chain IKEA planning to launch a new store in the Swedish town of Malmo turned to Facebook for promotion. IKEA set up a Facebook profile and uploaded pictures of several pieces of furniture in the store to the photo album. The company announced that the first person to tag his or her name to any piece would take home that article for free! On Facebook, the moment users tag something, everyone in their network gets to know about it.

So when people tagged themselves to the photos uploaded by IKEA, the word got around really fast through user profiles and Facebook news feeds. Soon, thousands of people flooded the IKEA page looking for freebies! The campaign was widely noticed in the blogosphere, generating immense publicity for the company. The smart social media campaign gave IKEA a good amount of publicity.

## Starbucks' status updates
The Starbucks fan page includes great videos and a variety of content geared to actively engage with fans. From the very beginning, Starbucks maintained a good frequency of updates with the aim of sharing something new in the form of videos, insightful blog posts, and articles about its employees as well as reviews of music and books on sale in their cafes.

The sheer volume and variety of the messages keeps its fans engaged. Each update invariably receives spontaneous comments. Status updates provide two-way communication between the company and its fans. The campaign amply establishes the fact that you need not use flashy applications to shine on Facebook. Just a regular dose of useful content can come in handy.

## Pringles' viral videos
Popular potato chip brand Pringles engages fans through reviews, discussions, and interactive games; it also makes great use of video on its fan page. Videos are one of the most commonly shared forms of online content and have greater chances of going 'viral'. Realizing that the audience relishes a touch of humor, the company has created a series of videos of people singing goofy songs. They put the videos on their page, giving fans a chance to share the videos with their friends and create a buzz about the brand, in the process.

The common denominator in all of the campaigns discussed above is their uniqueness in terms of creativity, interactivity and hence, the ability to engage with their audiences. The widespread reach of social media and its business-with-a-personal-touch aspect means that what the big boys can do, small businesses can well take a cue and follow suit.

## Small business successes
Facebook has turned into a popular medium for business promotion and thought leadership. The best part about it is that you don't need loads of cash to achieve success. Let's look at some enterprising people who are accomplishing their marketing goals through Facebook.

<u>The Equine Dentist</u>
Geoff Tucker is a Palm City, Florida-based equine dentist, who uses Facebook to generate leads for his business. Geoff has used Facebook to strike new relationships by befriending friends of friends. His mantra is that people like to do business with friends. Facebook also allows his clients to identify with Geoff and personally know him. The social media has virtually established him as a prominent thought leader in his business domain.

<u>T-Shirts with a message</u>
Rootsgear is an online apparel store, which designs T-shirts with political and social messages. Its company page on Facebook allows users to take a look at the designs as well as a calendar of the company's upcoming events. Rootsgear's Facebook page, which has over 5000 members, has driven an impressive flow of traffic and sales to its e-commerce site.

<u>Hooking steel customers</u>
Virginia-based SteelMaster, a manufacturer of prefabricated steel buildings, decided to create a Facebook fan page. It proved to be an excellent hook to engage existing customers. Pictures of select customers' sites ably demonstrated the company's execution capabilities and its wide range of buildings for prospective customers. Significantly, social media marketing provided SteelMaster with exposure to segments earlier not on its radar. For example, chicken farmers and woodworkers, generally avoiding steel buildings, got interested in the company and opened up a new business niche for it.

<u>A salon's social extensions</u>
If the experience of Seattle, Washington-based Emerson Salon is to be considered, it draws almost 75% of its business through social media. Its founders Matt Buchan and Alex Garcia have built an impressive online community from the outset. The Emerson Salon website is comprised of links to its social profiles on social networking platforms, blog feeds and even an online appointment button. Traffic to their website has tripled thanks to the social media initiative, the founders point out.

**In conclusion:**
Facebook is a powerful networking media that can connect you with people locally, nationally and worldwide - in different engaging ways. But you should follow certain norms for leveraging *The Mass Media of our Time!* We conclude by repeating a few of them.

1. Remember not to hard-sell your business on social media networks, from the word go...
2. Never tell people how great your product or service is. Rather tell them how excited you are about the product that you are working on currently and why. Update the company page regularly with insights into the product development process.
3. Make efforts to be genuine while talking about your products. You could share real experiences from people who have used your service or product. Be humble and genuine in your interactions.
4. Weave credible and real experiences around your brand or product to convey their intrinsic value. Keep in mind the fact that users respect authenticity and transparency on Facebook.
5. Your message should be special enough to draw everyone's attention. Instead of shooting off uninspiring messages, think differently to draw users to your page.

If you are still not on Facebook, you are clearly missing out on all the conversations, events, and networking opportunities that are happening here. Also, you are losing out on a lucrative business opportunity. So, what are you waiting for?

**In the next chapter:**
We shall talk about aspects like tweets, re-tweets, followers and other jargon related to Twitter – one of the most popular social media sites on the block. We shall examine strategies to leverage Twitter for a successful business presence, and review some success stories apart from referencing handy tools to help businesses to achieve success.

# Chapter 7

# Twitter

# Twitter: The Changing Face of Small Business Marketing

Twitter is now everywhere. Everyone from classes to masses is talking about it, and on it! Indeed, the social networking platform has emerged as one of the hottest communication trends today.

Launched in 2006, Twitter has pioneered the concept of micro-blogging. An online avenue for people to keep each other informed of their current status, it has fast evolved into a powerful social messaging platform, dramatically changing the way businesses market their products/services and communicate with customers.

Twitter has come as a boon, especially for small businesses with shoestring budgets. It's clearly forging a new era in brand promotion and marketing by enabling real-time communication at a minimal cost. Companies can gather vital feedback by enhancing engagement with customers.

It becomes possible to build lasting relationships with your key stakeholders and partners through sustained interactions thanks to Twitter. In essence, Twitter facilitates conversations and easy inflow of information, translating into a wider customer base and improved profit margins.

Twitter jargon: A peek
**Tweets:** Twitter allows members to send 140-character messages or updates called tweets the character limit allows tweets to be sent as mobile text messages. Your tweets will be displayed on your profile page and delivered to your subscribers, also known as 'followers'. You can 'follow' others and their corresponding tweets will show up in your timeline. The more people you 'follow', the more encompassing the tweet can be! (One downside though, sometimes following too many people can lead to clutter or even be considered spamming.) To reply to someone's twitter message, use the '@' sign followed by his or her name. For example, "@chrisbrogan Great article on adding tools to improve business."

The **RT**: (retweet) is a message that is repeated because you think it's noteworthy! When you retweet a message, it gets circulated among your 'followers'. For example, "RT @chrisbrogan Great article on adding tools to improve business."

**Shorturls:** The Twitter message space is constrained by the character limit, so you often need to convert long URLs into shorturls to fit in a message. You can use popular short url services like bit.ly and tinyurl to shorten the actual URL.

**Hash tags:** (#) are used to group tweets based on keywords. For example, using '#BarackObama' in a tweet lets everyone seeking content related to the President or his administration will come across this tweet.

**Direct messages:** (DMs) are private tweets that you can dispatch to your 'followers' using the 'message' link on your profile. You cannot send it to those not 'following' you.

For a small business owner, Twitter is indeed a remarkable tool that can help greatly expand its reach. It allows you to instantly connect with thousands of people, engage both existing and potential customers in a novel way.

## Setting up a business presence

Twitter is a great way to build your brand and give it a personality of its own! However, do not expect it to bring in immediate results in terms of sales. In the long term though, it sure can drive repeat customers. More importantly, Twitter offers you valuable insights into their mindsets and conveys their points of view to you so that you can customize your offerings. Your Followers may retweet your tweets along with their thoughts and opinions to people in their networks, thus widening your message base at no additional cost. Here are a few tips to enhance your presence on Twitter.

1. Your Twitter handle and profile should describe your area of focus on Twitter and the company or brand you represent.
2. Your bio should be as complete as possible – provide a link to your website, describe your business and put up a logo or other image. This will help your followers set their expectations accordingly.
3. It is better to use the name of your company in the handle, as this will help people easily find your brand. Preferably, try to keep the handle short as this helps in effective communication.
4. Be clear about whether the account will be maintained by one individual or a team of people within the company. Internally, define the roles and responsibilities that will be shared by your team.
5. All team members must be clear about the frequency of updates, how to respond in various situations and whom they should or should not follow or respond to.

Spend some time and explore the kind of content available on the networking service related to your industry. Search for your competitors to see if they are using Twitter, and if they are, discover what approaches they are taking so that you can devise your strategy, accordingly.

## Business strategies to succeed

This is what James Cameron, in one of his pre-Avatar interviews, said about Twitter: "There isn't one concept I would be interested in discussing with anyone that could be summed up in 25 words or fewer." In fact, this is exactly the hesitation and hurdle most small businesses face while using Twitter for marketing purposes. In this section, we will look at some key strategies that can help you leverage Twitter to help your business grow.

### Create conversations

Twitter helps companies to engage in real dialogues with people and enables companies quick feedback. You can ask your customers about their views on your product features and services. On Twitter, your followers will receive your query at once and can also provide immediate feedback. You can also ask your twitter community for suggestions on product/service enhancement or even promotion. The members will most likely reciprocate. Conversely, there will be people asking questions related to your industry. Relieving their doubts will help build your company's credibility.

### Stay in touch

It is important to stay in touch with your Twitter contacts. You can share interesting links and useful industry-related information within your network. Plan a regular schedule of meet-ups (or as many like to call it, tweetups!) with your local Twitter followers; make announcements about upcoming company events or workshops; provide live updates during such events. This will lend visibility to your brand. Contests are a popular way to create awareness about your brand. Conduct your own contest on Twitter to build excitement and grow your followers.

### Establish expertise

Be up-to-date with all your industry news; use # hashtag searches to get all the breaking news from your business domain. Share them on your Twitter account. This will arouse interest among your followers, who will be keen to connect. On your part, search for the influencers such as industry experts, bloggers, etc. within your industry and follow them. You can send them direct messages (DMs) too.

### Promotions

Post links of recent blog posts about your industry as well as website updates through tweets. This will help drive more traffic. If you have submitted your blog posts to sites like Digg and delicious, you can tweet these links to increase their popularity and traffic.

Monitor brand mentions
As a small business, it is in your best interest to keep track of what people are saying about your brand on Twitter. Use #yourcompanyname searches to check for such mentions, and make a point to reply to individuals curious about your brand! If there is a complaint, take steps to address it immediately. In case of praise and applause, send a direct Thank You message (DM) to the individual. Your quick response will tell people that you are willing to listen and respond to them. Ensure that your tweets are representative of your company's culture and working philosophy, or else there will be a jarring disconnect.

Research and relation building tool
Utilize Twitter to promote a new product or service or to announce a sale and get the word out fast. Twitter is also a great medium to manage a PR crisis. In case of any complaint, immediately get on Twitter, and explain your side of the story. Share ways to be accountable. With Twitter, you can do good damage control. Twitter is also a great tool for market research. You can conduct polls and surveys, ask questions and follow niche topics.

Contact journalists and bloggers
Online communities value a friend's word over any kind of advertisement or press release. You can take advantage of this by contacting journalists who cover your industry or influential bloggers and asking them if they would be keen to review your products or services. Be sure to send a direct message (DM) or email them first to check whether they are interested before tweeting them.

**The best apps**
One of the main engines fueling the explosive growth of Twitter is that users can post and view tweets through several different ways. You can use desktop-based applications like TweetDeck or use the Web to manage your Twitter account or post tweets from your mobile phone. It has been noticed that a significant percentage of tweets come from sources other than Twitter.com. There are several useful applications that do the job much better than the standard Twitter interface. In this section, we will discuss some of the most popular online applications that add functionality to your Twitter experience.

TweetDeck
TweetDeck is a very popular desktop app to access Twitter. TweetDeck increases your experience in several ways: it allows you to organize your followers into specific categories, it has better video playback, it auto-suggests usernames, integrates yfrog (which allows you to share images and videos with ease), and with TweetDeck

you can have unlimited columns. The iPhone app is complementary. Recent updates allow maps, URL shorteners, scheduling updates, integrating Foursquare and Google Buzz as well as uploading video to TwitVid from file or through webcam.

Twitter for iPhone
Tweetie, considered the top mobile application, is now called Twitter for iPhone. Twitter for iPhone allows you a great view of conversations. It helps manage multiple accounts, save searches and even post videos to yfrog. It's a single column app with multiple account management capabilities and boasts of functional conversation threads. However, it lacks the groups feature.

Seesmic
Seesmic is a feature-rich, easy to use application. It supports unlimited Twitter accounts and columns, URL and photo options; has great Facebook integration and unlimited saved searchism and lets you see your followersand drag users from one list to another. You can easily 'follow' or 'unfollow' users, share photos and post videos to YouTube. You can share links from bit.ly and view your Direct Messages (DMs) in a simple threaded view. You can also see the conversation thread clearly, allowing for easy replies.

Hootsuite
Hootsuite is a web-based app with an easy-to-use interface to manage multiple Twitter profiles, add multiple editors and pre-schedule tweets. It's a multiple column app with a very good groups feature. You can upload pictures and files, save searches, track analytics as well as reply and send messages to people on your lists. It also offers an iPhone app.

CoTweet
CoTweet enables companies to engage in proactive marketing and response-oriented customer service activities. It allows multiple people to manage a single account and avoids duplication of effort. It enables users to schedule tweets, assign tweets to co-workers, and add notes for Twitter users.

The best way to identify the app suited to your requirements is to experiment and find out what works for you! Once you have found the right app, you can look forward to an enhanced and a far more productive Twitter experience.

**Successful case studies**
Corporations are looking for new ways to sell products/services and engage with their consumers. They are increasingly turning to social media to create brand

awareness, ensure engagement and facilitate quick service. We shall now look at companies and brands that have utilized Twitter to run some successful campaigns.

## Zappos' personality drives brand

The Amazon-owned online retailer Zappos is one of the best examples of companies to have pioneered the usage of Twitter for corporate interaction. The credit goes to its CEO Tony Hsieh, who has used his Twitter account to lend a friendly, helpful and trustworthy touch to the brand. He is comfortable interacting with a new technology and sharing behind-the-scenes information. He even encourages employees to have active accounts so that they use Twitter to talk to their customers. The Zappos site has a page that aggregates all the Twitter streams. Such micro-interaction along with an emphasis on customer service has created word-of-mouth benefits and has fetched rich rewards for the brand.

## Ford's successful usage of Twitter

The automaker knows a thing or two about social media. The Ford Fiesta Movement was a grassroots social media campaign to promote the new model by giving away Ford Fiestas to 100 influential bloggers and asking them to share their experiences through Twitter, blogs, videos and events. The campaign generated over 3 million Twitter impressions in just six months. Ford credited social media, notably Twitter, for success while not spending a dollar on traditional advertising. With its Fiesta campaign, Ford showed social media is not about 'the company talking about its brand;' it's more about 'making the people talk about your brand.'

## Comcast offers customer support via Twitter

Comcast is using Twitter to offer excellent customer service to consumers as well as monitoring complaints about their service thanks to Frank Eliason, the man behind @comcastcares, a Twitter account that aims to help Comcast users in need. The point to be made here is that, having a Twitter account is not good enough. The next logical step is to use it to monitor online conversations about your products/services or brand. This will enable you to offer better customer service, resulting in better brand loyalty.

## Best Buy links real-time service

Consumer electronics retailer Best Buy understood that people sometimes find it challenging to learn the details of product features so it encouraged its sales and tech support staff to handle online customer service and company promotions through a service called Twelpforce on Twitter. The idea was to invite customers to be part of conversations and to offer real-time customer service. People can submit questions directly to Twelpforce and any Best Buy employee will reply to the customer. Twelpforce has helped humanize the company and established Best Buy as a brand that listens to its customers, provides real-time interaction and shares useful tips and advice about technology.

Jet Blue flies high
Jet Blue was one of the first major brands to join Twitter. The original idea was to just help its customers. Through a hit and miss process, the company discovered what really worked on Twitter and what didn't! For example, chatty posts and customer service assistance generated instantaneous replies and new followers. The company is often cited as an example of smart corporate twittering.

**Small business successes**
Curiously, small businesses have been a bit more circumspect about using Twitter for business promotion and creating a customer relationship, though businesses do not need big budgets to create a successful marketing campaign on Twitter. Let's check out a few small businesses that have jumped onto the social media bandwagon and managed to trump up their products and services.

CoffeeGroundz
Houston, Texas-based CoffeeGroundz is a small but popular independent coffee shop, selling a variety of locally roasted coffee, tea, pastries and sandwiches. In October 2008, its general manager J R Cohen went on Twitter. Within a short span of time, he realized the importance of Twitter to his business. Cohen made a genuine effort to connect with each individual customer following him on Twitter. His twitter followers are also encouraged to place orders, reserve a table/booth, order from the patio, or reserve the place for events on Twitter through direct messages. In fact, CoffeeGroundz is credited with the first To-Go Order placed on Twitter. CoffeeGroundz customer Sean Stoner was hungry and so he tweeted the following message to Cohen:

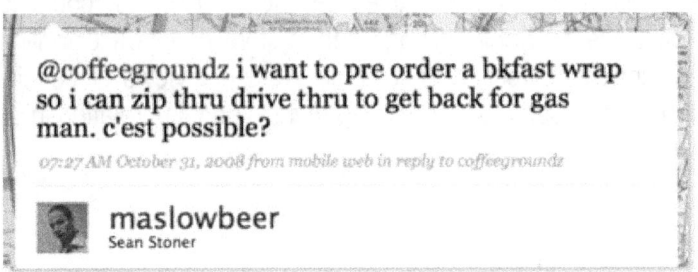

Cohen quickly responded and Sean picked up his burrito through the drive-thru at CoffeeGroundz.

> @maslowbeer Wi. What do you want on it?
> 07:28 AM October 31, 2008 from web in reply to maslowbeer
>
>  coffeegroundz

### Feather Your Nest with connections

Arkansas-based Feather Your Nest is a specialty shop for homemade and vintage-looking gifts. Web-savvy owner Gina Drennon took her business online and used Twitter to stand out from the crowd in her tourist resort town of Eureka Springs. The town boasts an array of such shops but very few owners have an online presence. Feather Your Nest has had tremendous success – not just in terms of website hits and sales increases. Gina's Twitter account, which has over 2,000 followers, has helped her build connections with bloggers and magazine editors, who have featured the owner and her company.

### Sushi restaurant Umi

Shamus Booth is the co-owner of Umi, a sushi restaurant in San Francisco. He sometimes gets five new customers a night who have heard about it on Twitter. Shamus twitters about the fresh fish of the night – "The O-Toro (bluefin tuna belly) tonight is some of the most rich and buttery tuna I've had." He also offers free seaweed salads to people who mention Twitter.

### Liberty Bay Books relationships

Liberty Bay Books, an independent bookstore located in Poulsbo, Washington, specializes in Scandinavian and nautical books. Its owner Suzanne Droppert says that social media enables her to share views and ideas with her customers as well as with the authors who visit her store. She uses her store's Twitter account to discuss books, food, local events, book signings and in-store events. Her online conversations reflect her sincere interest in her customers and their views. Her social media efforts have led to an increase in sales and a growth in genuine relationships with her customers.

**In conclusion:**
Small businesses with a shoestring marketing budget should never underestimate the power of word of mouth generated by social networking platforms like Twitter. Businesses are able to obtain a growing number of customers through this word of mouth advertising. In fact, Twitter's short character format encourages people to spread news to friends in their own network. Every business, big or small, can work toward initiating conversations and building connections with their customers.

You can build a brand personality by sharing significant links and information related to your industry, discussing relevant topics and responding to people's queries and suggestions politely and positively. During the entire communication chain, you must be receptive to what your followers want. You can then gauge their responses to your tweets and take necessary steps to build your brand.

By focusing on creating unique content, having one-to-one conversations and providing immediate service to customers, your business can build a lasting online reputation thanks to Twitter.

**In the next chapter:**
We shall introduce readers to LinkedIn and how to take advantage of the networking site for professionals, including personal branding, business networking and job opportunities. We shall discuss aspects like creating a profile, adding and managing connections as well as using its other sections. We will also talk about things that you must avoid on LinkedIn. Last but not least, you will learn about the various strategies to leverage LinkedIn through Search Engine Optimization (SEO) techniques.

# Chapter 8

## Linkedin

# LinkedIn for Business Networking

LinkedIn, launched in May 2003, has now become an extremely popular social networking platform among businesses and professionals. It allows users to create business contacts, find potential clients and search for jobs.

**An important resource for business opportunities**
There is no doubt about the fact that LinkedIn is a fast-growing network with enormous potential. It can be a valuable resource to you and your business. Whether you are a job seeker or an entrepreneur, this networking site can act as a big boost. Through LinkedIn, you can widen the scope of your professional network and leverage the capabilities of other professionals.

Compared to other social networking sites, there is relatively less clutter on LinkedIn pages and hence it appeals to the 'professional' audience. However, just like any other social media marketing initiative, you have to stay proactive and strike a chord with the people you wish to connect with on the network. Let's look at how LinkedIn can help you become better networked:

Company profile as resume
You can create a company profile with information about your company and a list of all your employees. This will make it easier for people to know more about your business and the quality of personnel. You can also use your company profile as a tool for reputation management if required.

Connect with industry leaders
LinkedIn can help you identify influential people within your industry and get in touch with them. You can approach them for possible business ventures or product reviews or even to write an article for your blog as a guest blogger.

Stay in touch with other professionals
LinkedIn is an easy way to stay in touch with colleagues, industry peers, or people you happen to meet at an official event or convention. Unlike other social networks, LinkedIn has a clean interface, which allows users to check your professional growth and history with ease.

Effective Search Engine Optimization (SEO)
LinkedIn is very SEO friendly. A quick Google search often throws up LinkedIn profiles right on top of the results page. This can make it easy for peers and prospects to find you.

Poll, Survey and Testimonials
You can ask peers and influencers like bloggers to write recommendations and testimonials. These can be powerful in establishing your reputation in the industry. Another way to get involved is to run a poll or survey or ask questions to your peers. Also, reciprocate by answering peer queries yourself.

**How to get started**
LinkedIn, as we have already found out, is a great place to develop your budding business, grow your capabilities and promote your projects, and look for lucrative opportunities. With its vast networking capabilities, and application-rich features, LinkedIn is certainly a powerful tool to maintain and establish relationships in the business world. It can also be handy to attract top talent to your company.

Remember, your LinkedIn profile is your professional portrait, so make sure that it is complete. Let's now grasp the nuances of creating a catchy profile.

Personal Profile
To get started, create a personal profile to add a list of contacts, connect with old colleagues or schoolmates, and build a network for your business. For your profile, enter your personal and professional information – make sure that the profile is available to the public. Personalize your profile URL using your name, as this makes it look more professional. Opt for the 'full view' of your profile. Check and add all requisite information in the relevant boxes. The summary should highlight your professional capabilities – it should not only be about what you are doing, but also about what you are capable of doing.

Be specific about the company you work for - whether as employee or an entrepreneur. Mention your company's primary focus so that others can see what you bring to the table along with your personal skills. Write briefly about your academic and professional background, including work experience. If possible, seek recommendations from your clients or people you know to maximize your exposure on the LinkedIn network. Add relevant sites to your profile. Customize the URLs by choosing 'other' in the edit section and adding the anchor text. This helps get better search results.

Company Profile
As a business owner, a company page is good to find work and important connections. Add a company page to your LinkedIn profile. Enter a brief introduction about the company, its domain and the number of employees it has. Add the company logo and a feed for your company or personal blog. You can get your employees to link

to this page. Add a 'Follow' button on the page, so that your connections can know about all that's happening in your company. For example, a hiring exercise, recent research and polls, as well as new products or services can all be featured here!

The description copy should highlight what your company does and must contain the right keywords to make it search engine friendly. Add websites as well as a news module about the happenings in your company or the industry. Once your company profile is set up, LinkedIn will pull in data about your company from the site. You can also get enhanced features to add videos, interactive polls, and other options for recruiting as needed. To start with, a basic LinkedIn company profile should suffice for most small businesses.

## The strategies
Small businesses can utilize LinkedIn to connect with companies or influential individuals and network for business opportunities. While connecting with people, make sure that they are relevant to your business. Write a personal message when sending out invitations. Allow your personal style to come through in the profile. Keep all LinkedIn conversations professional and use it as a platform for personal branding, networking discussions, and establishing yourself as an authority in your area of expertise.

Let's discuss how to brand your profile. Here are some key strategies that will help you leverage your LinkedIn profile to gain attention and enhance your business prospects.

### Personal branding
**Custom URL:** You can customize your profile URL by using the Edit function on your profile settings. Replace the default URL with your name – for example, linkedin.com/in/johnsmith – so that search engines can easily find your page and rank you higher on the search results. If your name happens to be already taken, then you could try adding a period like linkedin.com/in/john.smith

**Headline:** Do not leave the default headline, which automatically displays the last job you held. Revise your profile headline to position yourself as an expert in your field.

**Summary:** Your summary should be a small paragraph about your work experience, unique abilities and achievements, as well as a brief mention of your company and its goals. Use keywords in your summary to make it easier for search engines to find you.

**List your websites:** LinkedIn allows you to list three websites on your profile. Take advantage of that space and advertise anything associated with your company website, a blog or even your social networking profile. Select 'Other' while adding the list, as this will allow you to add titles to your links. This will add to the search engine optimization of these websites simply by being listed here.

**Recommendations:** Try to add at least three recommendations to your LinkedIn profile. These recommendations will always work in your favour.

Position yourself as a leader
**Start a group:** Starting a LinkedIn group and initiating thoughtful discussions will always help establish your credentials as an industry leader or even trendsetter. Begin a LinkedIn group based upon a topic and not your company; it can be localized to your city/region. Check profiles of your current contacts to see if the group is relevant to their respective interests and then invite them. Promote the group on other social media platforms where you have a presence, to add members initially. Deliver news content, useful articles and discussions – these will help you grow your community. Also, syndicate your blog through LinkedIn to bring in additional traffic.

**Start an event:** LinkedIn events are held only for professional interests or conferences and can help you become a niche leader. Start your own networking event and promote it to your current LinkedIn audience along with your second and third degree contacts.

**Ask and answer questions:** If someone asks a question regarding your area of expertise, make it a point to answer back. In this way, you will be perceived as a contributor and someone who will help out others when required. You can also initiate a LinkedIn Poll and target professionals with the right expertise.

Business networking
Developing your business network means that your direct connections as well as the second and third degree contacts are visible and always in a position to help.

**Import your contacts:** While building your network, use the import function to import contacts from Windows Live, Hotmail, Gmail, Yahoo! and AOL. Add your colleagues or friends from other companies to increase your contacts.

**Readily accept contact requests:** Always make yourself available to accept contact requests and continue conversations to help build relationships. Make your email address public on your profile so that people can add you to their network.

**Promote your URL:** Promote your personal LinkedIn URL as your email signature, on your resume, blog, website, presentations and business card.

**Status message:** Maintain professionalism in your LinkedIn status messages, keeping in mind your network audience.

SEO strategy
Most often, people, who wish to work with you, will conduct an online search for your LinkedIn profile that will show up in the results. Your LinkedIn profile, if properly optimized, can provide SEO-friendly links because search engines like Google find it easy to index LinkedIn. In the case of a keyword match, your LinkedIn profile will invariably be displayed on the search results page. You also have the option to add unique anchor text to your website or blog links. For this, go to the Websites section under Edit My Profile and select 'Other' in the drop down box. This gives you an extra box to put in your keyword title along with your website URL. You can add up to 3 sites which you can use to promote your business website and even blogs. These are valuable links that contribute to your backlinks and give you good page ranks on search engines. You can also connect your blog RSS feed to your profile, which will automatically present your new posts on LinkedIn.

Job opportunities
While posting a job to LinkedIn, provide details about the position, skills and requirements. Your company profile will provide potential candidates with relevant information about your company. Interested candidates can look at your employees' list and check if any of them are second or third degree connections, in which case, they can ask their contacts for an introduction.

**Things to avoid**
Irregular status updates
If you do not update your status regularly, people will think you are inactive, marking you as an infrequent visitor to the page. Regularly post updates and let people know what you are doing, reading or travelling. Your status update must be appealing to read. It should inform about your latest activities as well as add value to your branding on LinkedIn. Your status posts will act as first impressions for companies or prospects looking for you online.

SEO-unfriendly summary
Your profile summary offers scope for personal branding and making sure that any keywords associated with you are easily found. This space can be utilized to tell everyone who you are and what your capabilities are as a professional!

### Not putting up your photo
Putting up your personal photo lends credibility to your profile. You want people to know you as a real person and convey to them that it's not a fake profile! Use a professional headshot for the profile – avoid using old pictures and pictures of family or pets.

### Bland profile headline
Your profile headline appears next to your name in search results and next to any questions you ask or answer. The headline is very important. Avoid writing your position or the name of your company there. Use it as your branding pitch.

### Not listing all companies or schools
Listing all the schools and colleges you have attended and all the companies you have worked for over the years makes it easier to find you on LinkedIn. If you have missed out on listing even one of these, you are missing out on some valuable connections. Especially, you must list all the companies with which you are now or have been associated since there could be a colleague trying to connect with you!

### Missing job descriptions
So you have now listed positions for all the companies for which you have previously worked. The next important step is to add job descriptions. They give a good scope for adding keywords to your profile, which will help in optimizing the page for search engines. Do not miss out on this!

### Fewer connections
The more connections you have the more search results you will appear in. Don't know whom to add? You can add connections by joining various relevant groups and connecting with the members.

### Avoid product promotion in discussions
Do not begin your sales pitch right after connecting with a person or after joining a group discussion. You run the risk of being tagged as a spammer. Keeping it low-key is the rule of the game on LinkedIn. Exploit group discussions more to establish yourself as an expert resource and not to promote yourself or your products/sevices, at least in the beginning.

### Do not join too many groups
Group discussions can be a magnet for drawing positive attention. However, by joining too many groups, you are in danger of having no dedicated time to adequately participate in specific groups. Join two or three relevant groups that can help you

connect with potential customers or partners.

Lack of testimonials
This is especially important for small business owners. When describing a product or service, be sure to explain its benefits. Also get your customers to write as many positive reviews of your company on your profile. This adds to your credibility.

**Case Studies: At a glance**
Power of groups, keywords
Thomas Merlino in Erie, Pennsylvania decided to start a small business called InControl Technical in 2007. It intended to provide technical services locally. To connect with other professionals and business owners in the region, Thomas created a group on LinkedIn called LinkedErie. Along with other businessmen, the aspiring entrepreneur uses the group to promote his business, network with peers as well as connect with current and potential customers. By populating his LinkedIn profile with proper keywords, Thomas Merlino has been able to attract business from his locality as well as outside.

Great tool for job searches
Kathy Robinson, the former HR executive who runs TurningPoint Career Consulting, says that with its access to contacts, groups, events, and thought leaders, LinkedIn has proved to be a great tool for job seekers. Groups can help you initiate a conversation. She helps job seekers optimize their profiles to network with as many groups as possible. Her clients have received excellent offers thanks to online networking.

Gain market awareness
Austin Arensberg, who works for a private renewable energy investment fund, has used LinkedIn to identify potential investment prospects. He uses LinkedIn to gain market knowledge; meet key contacts; participate in group discussions; and attend local conferences and events to increase networking opportunities, which can lead to potential investment options. For example, when he needed information about companies building renewable energy power projects in China, he joined a relevant group in LinkedIn and initiated a discussion about investment proposals. Within hours, he had connected with professionals boasting expertise of working in the industry in China.

Fundraising for Startups
Irish startup Goshido, a management consulting firm, raised $230,000 just by

utilizing LinkedIn contacts. What's more, they raised the funds within eight days! The company searched for potential investors on LinkedIn and sent about 700 messages. They received 200 responses from potential investors, within a week. CEO Frank Hannigan considers LinkedIn the "largest collection of trust agents" in the world.

## Polls help gather useful info
Philadelphia-based Linda Chell Rooney, a partner at Beacon-Point Associates, used the Polls application to gather ideas for a teleseminar series on issues in home construction and real estate. Within a month, she received about 100 responses. She also promoted the seminars on LinkedIn and attracted several participants.

## Integrated marketing plan
Kathy Steele, who works at an integrated marketing firm, credits LinkedIn with changing their entire business process. Using LinkedIn, the firm leverages the experience of group members, creates new connections, evaluates ideas and stays in touch with current relationships to increase sales and advertise achievements. The company also uses LinkedIn to communicate. Its experience shows that the professional network brings in better and quicker responses compared to emails or phones. The company also reviews a contact's LinkedIn profile before a meeting to be more prepared.

**In conclusion:**
Social media messaging takes time and commitment, especially for professional purposes. But the returns can be handsome. Ultimately, you can be assured of credible visibility and several lucrative opportunities to present your capabilities to interested prospects.

By having an active LinkedIn profile, every update will remind people of your presence and activities. This will help you in networking with more people online. Make sure your profile as well as profiles of your key team members is regularly updated. Your profile must reflect a professional message. Use your LinkedIn network to gain new leads, connect with more people and showcase your industry expertise to gain more exposure. This is bound to boost your professional credentials.

**In the next chapter:**

We shall discuss various types of videos, strategies to market videos on the web andways to track the success of your videos.

# Chapter 9

# Video
# (You Tube, Animoto, etc.)

# Videos – New frontier in Online Marketing

There have been several dramatic changes in the way we assimilate information. In 2004, broadband was slowly getting popular, but watching videos online was still some time away. Primarily because videos were shared through emails and either your mailbox got clogged trying to download huge attachments (video files were heavier) or your system would shutdown trying to play one. Then in 2006, YouTube was launched and suddenly videos became exciting. People could now send links to websites and blogs other than YouTube that had embedded videos hosted by the platform. Soon watching videos online became an essential part of the experience. As businesses began using the power of the Internet, online videos began to be part of marketing strategies.

Ignoring the use of videos for your business can make it seem invisible. Videos help start a relationship between a company and its customers. Videos can bring ideas to life and grab attention right away. The medium can help create a viral buzz around a product or service. It can tell a story in minutes and is worth more than a 1000 pictures. If your viewers love a video, they will expect similar videos from you and will continue to visit your site, thus driving increased traffic.

Video is, perhaps, the most underutilized Social Media marketing strategy. It can be a very powerful tool for businesses, big or small. Small businesses may be intimidated to create videos, but there is no need to be. And budgets are not more important than creative ideas. After all, having a budget video is better than not having a video at all. Let's discuss what kind of videos will help drive traffic to your business and websites.

### Types of videos
Small businesses can create online video to enhance corporate branding, viral marketing, public relations and educational efforts. The subject of each video as well as its distribution will depend on your marketing goal and budget. The Internet evolution has created several free and low-cost tools, which can be used by small businesses to create and promote online videos. Videos help businesses to raise their brand awareness as well as increase interaction with current and potential customers.

Videos can be of a lecture series or simply zany viral videos, which don't directly promote your business or brand but will rather create general awareness of your brand. To succeed, viral videos should be original, unusual, unexpected and funny.

Viral videos are a great way to raise interest before a product launch as they can direct visitors to your site.

For brand marketing, you can create a welcome video for your websites, video testimonials from customers or email marketing initiatives. It always helps to hear from satisfied customers and clients. You could even keep a simple camera in the office/store to record instant testimonials. You could add a video tour of your office or facility on your website or blog. Seeing your office or store gives the client a personal connection with your business. You can also initiate a spotlight series featuring an employee or a customer every month. On your websites, add video recaps of events, meetings and trade shows attended by you or your company and include videos of your speaking engagements.

You can create interesting video blogs (vlogs) and attention-grabbing contests as well as promote success stories to showcase your product or service using promotional videos. Videos are also a great public relations tool. You can create and distribute video news releases, statements from company leaders, discussions with industry leaders, and you can promote any company media interviews. If a tips section is relevant to your products, showcase these through videos – it will hold people's interest as well as help build a positive perception about your company. The how-to videos can be about a favorite recipe, ways to braid hair or shop for furniture or insurance. You can create a video to put up product tutorials and demonstrations and show potential customers how to use your products. You can even offer basic customer and technical support solutions in video.

## Online video strategy
Video is a compelling medium and a great way to engage your customers. You can either use a third party site to host your videos or host them yourself. Let's take a look at the steps you need to take to create a video strategy for your website.

### Select a hosting platform
For smaller businesses, it is recommended to use a third party site because hosting it yourself involves a lot of technical know-how including file hosting, player selection and customization, tracking analytics and bandwidth costs. Third party platforms can offer you better bandwidth costs and offers you tools to manage your video. However, if you are looking to monetize your video ads, increase brand awareness or looking for a complete video platform to boost your business goals, it is better to go for a mixed strategy. YouTube, DailyMotion and Animoto are among some of the more popular web hosting platforms.

**YouTube:** YouTube, often synonymous with online videos, is a video-sharing website where users can upload, share, and view videos. Launched in 2005, Google purchased it for $1.65 billion and now operates as a Google subsidiary. The California-based company displays a wide variety of user-generated video content, including movie clips, TV clips, music videos and amateur content like video blogs and original videos.

**Animoto:** Animoto is an application that streams together your photos, video clips and music into professional videos in minutes. Animoto is a step up from boring slideshow presentations. The site, launched in 2007, had over 1 million users by November 2009 while its Facebook application has been used by over two million.

**Dailymotion:** Dailymotion is a video sharing service website, based in Paris, France. As of January 2008, the site received about 16,000 new videos daily. As of April 2009, the site has been getting over 55 million unique monthly visitors who viewed approximately 17 billion pages since the start of that year.

Irrespective of the third party host you choose to post your video, remember the content and description is important. Pay good attention to these and ensure that they convey the message of the video as well as complement your company's values. Videos on third party sites must carry the URL information of your websites so that users know where they can go to get more information.

Opt for a hybrid strategy
You can put a preview video on YouTube with the complete video on your site – the preview clip will be a teaser and encourage viewers to visit your site for the complete content. Also, YouTube compresses videos to a lower quality, so you can offer a high definition version on your site; this is especially important if the content is entertainment-based content and will be better enjoyed in full screen mode. In the video description, provide additional relevant information, like articles, case studies or contests that are available on your site. This will encourage people to visit your site for details. You can also put the same video on both YouTube and your site.

Set up a channel
Set up a channel on a video sharing site of your choice. Fill out your profile with information that will help users to understand your brand. Organize your content to give you credibility. Communicate and participate in related communities or channels to improve your visibility and increase traffic share to your site.

## Optimize your video

The more you optimize a video; the easier it will be for users to find the video on the search engine results page. If your videos are not optimized well, they will get pushed farther down by content that boast better search syntax. Let's explore some ways that you can optimize your videos:

- Ensure flexibility in video formats. Offer your videos in multiple formats to make it more accessible to users;
- Your videos must have a compelling summary. The summary should convince users to click on them;
- Apply SEO principles to optimize your videos – assign keywords to your videos after conducting proper research;
- You can embed links to relevant videos in your online press releases;
- Promote videos on your website. Do you have a video testimonial or a video endorsement of your products or services? You can feature these video links on your website homepage;
- Enable 'share' options on all your videos so that viewers can easily share them. Videos can easily become viral content;

Some other ways to optimize your videos are discussed below:

### Filenames

Give proper filenames to the images and video files you use for any online marketing strategy – search engines will fail to recognize random filenames. So use descriptive names for videos like keynote-speech-at-carolina-startup-meet.mp4, which help video SEO.

### Brand visibility

Add your branding to every video. The company logo or a small message can be shown before the video rolls or used like a sub-title or as a backdrop to the video. People on video sharing sites like to embed or share videos so, when they do, your branding will let more people know about your company, brand, or website URL.

### Call-to-action in videos

Prompt users for another action after watching the videos. Ask them to visit your website, or a link to learn more or a link to related videos on your site. Call–to-action links must always indicate what the user will get when they reach your site. Call-to-action links and content will help search engines understand the context of your video.

### Clear audio

A clear audio will help generate automated video transcripts that are accurate and of good quality. This will help in video SEO and make it easy for users to understand the content.

### Shorter videos
Keeping your videos to 10 minutes or less will help the viewer to better understand your content with greater visual impact. Shorter videos also help minimize bandwidth costs.

### The metadata
Metadata is an important part of your video strategy. Captions and other text elements in your videos can help both users and search engines to identify content and pull results.

### Text
Every video should have a catchy, yet descriptive title and description. Complete all information fields as this helps in video search. Pick and focus on select keywords while writing titles, description and tags. This makes it easier for users to find your videos and they also help your videos to rank higher on search results. Choose keywords that are relevant to the video and to your target audience. Do not go overboard with keyword usage. Remember, video is an interesting medium, so avoid using dry language while writing descriptions – keep it short, funny and creative.

### Related text
Provide related video links and content around each video. For an interview, adding a transcript or related articles is a great idea as this will help search engines to understand and index your videos and your users to easily understand the content.

### Thumbnail
This is a still image taken from a video to compel the viewer to click. Pick an image that best summarizes your video.

### Video sitemap
This helps to increase your chances of your video showing up in Google search results. You can go to Google Webmaster Support for more information. You can also use MRSS, similar to blog RSS, which submits your feed to Google as soon as you publish a new video.

Once the video is uploaded on the channel or the webpage with appropriate content, start looking at the views it garners to measure its success. More than that, several platforms offer detailed metrics to measure and track the effectiveness of your video strategy.

## YouTube strategies

YouTube, which serves more than a billion videos per day, has become the go-to video site for millions of users across the web. It can also be an effective Social Media marketing strategy. YouTube's free-to-use model, ease of use and mass market audience makes it a great channel for small businesses. But it must be used appropriately to get the most out of it. Let's take a look at some dos and don'ts that can help small businesses take the utmost advantage of YouTube.

## Create and customize your channel

Set up your YouTube channel, add your company's branding, modify the colors to reflect your company's look, and add relevant information and links. Take advantage of the option to subscribe to your channel. YouTube also allows you to highlight just uploads, playlists, favorites or all.

### Subtitles

Add subtitles by using YouTube's auto-captioning. Captions will help in easy understanding of the audio making your content accessible to anyone keen to watch it. Edit the copy for accuracy.

### Tagging

Add the correct tags to your videos. Try to use the most relevant tags, but you can also experiment with a variety of tags. Monitor the performance of different videos to check the effectiveness of your tagging system and, accordingly, make changes in the future.

### Playlists and folders

Make your channel viewer-friendly by creating playlists to group together relevant videos. Archive your videos using time-related or subject-related folders. You can embed individual videos or entire playlists into external sites, so ensure accuracy of titles and descriptions.

### Remove offensive comments

Act decisively to stop people from posting spam or comments that use offensive language to your videos or channel. Don't take down any negative or critical comments, especially if they are relevant to the subject on hand. You can also block any user who keeps posting spam or offensive remarks. Opt for moderation of comments so you can approve them before they go live.

### Interact with the community

Be active on other channels of your interest, 'favorite' relevant videos and make suitable 'friends'. You can associate with other companies, or channels, covering your city or region or a good cause that you/your company supports.

Video promotion
Each time you post a video, embed it in your blog, your Facebook Page or twitter feed about it. If selected, YouTube's account setting automatically publishes the new video to your social network accounts. This will help push users towards your video content. Allow users to embed your videos on other external sites – this will bring in additional traffic.

Analytics
YouTube offers free analytics data via the "Insight" button on every uploaded video. It can offer some valuable information on views statistics, demographics, community, as well as details about how various users came across the video.

Don't neglect your channel
Just like any other Social Media marketing method, do not let your enthusiasm to post videos on YouTube decline after a few months. If you are committed to this strategy, continue to post content or just keep the account active by commenting, accepting friends or adding favorites.

**Track the success of your videos**
Tracking your videos' statistics is important as it allows you to monitor the efforts and initiatives that are working and the ones that are not working. This is imperative to promote your business through a video strategy. Also, tracking helps isolate popular keywords that people are using in search engines to look for your industry or niche. You can track your videos statistics using YouTube. Video analytics tool YouTube Insight provides detailed metrics on video views and activity for all users. To view reports, click your username on your YouTube account. Select 'My videos' and on the subsequent page, select 'Insight'. This will take you to your report with information about your click-through rates, the number of hits for your video, the visitor demographics and popularity of your video.

Google Analytics is also a great way to track and measure traffic to YouTube brand channels. Google Analytics answers your queries about how your visitors found your channel, the amount of time spent on your channel, your visitor demographics and the extent of their repeat visits. To begin with, you have to sign up for a Google Analytics account. Once you have added all requisite fields of information, it will take 24 hours for data to appear in your account. To view reports, log in to your analytics account and access the data collected on your channel.

# Success stories

## A YouTube makeover
Lauren Luke was selling cosmetics on Ebay when she registered with YouTube and began filming make-up tutorials after her buyers requested her for beauty advice. She offers a step-by-step guide to achieve almost any look, but her video about getting the 'Leona Lewis look' was the breakthrough moment. That video got massive hits and brought in a new wave of viewers to her channel. So far, she has had over 34 million hits. By 2008, UK based make-up brand, Barry M signed her up to create exclusive make-up looks with their products on YouTube.

## Blend it on!
Social Media marketing doesn't always cost a lot of money. The "Will It Blend?" series on YouTube was a viral marketing campaign comprising a series of infomercials for the Blendtec line of blenders. In the videos, Blendtec CEO Tom Dickson attempts to blend various items to show off the power of the blender. It was a low-cost marketing campaign which leveraged YouTube's subscriber base. By creating a fun and original series, Blendtec had a successful campaign in their hands which importantly led to a "five-fold increase in sales."

## Man up with YouTube
The Social Man, a New York City-based small social coaching business, has its own YouTube channel. The firm runs its "Ask the Social Man" series in which Hudson and his colleagues answer questions on dating and pick-up techniques. Founder Jonathan Christian Hudson says that videos were a great way to have a real dialog with their clients and prospects. And the casual tone of the conversation by the coaches makes them relatable to their audiences. After uploading daily videos, the company has seen a rise in site traffic and sales.

## Stringing it along
John W. Tuggle, a guitarist from Athens, Georgia had been playing guitar and giving private lessons for about 15 years. So he wrote a "how to" book and created a website to sell it. The venture failed. Realizing that he will have to market beyond his local area, he built a YouTube channel, a blog, a podcast, offered digital downloads and live Skype lessons. Within a few months, Gibson Guitars discovered John on YouTube and added him as a recommended instructor on their website. Instead of playing gigs and being a studio engineer, John was now teaching students, and even had a few from overseas. He's the very definition of a small business online marketing success story.

A hit flight safety video?
Delta Airlines produced an in-flight safety demonstration video, featuring a real employee, which was then posted on YouTube, even before it debuted on an actual flight. The campaign was a huge success, garnered free media attention, and the video got over one million views. It was a cheap and easy way for Delta to accomplish its goal of promoting passenger safety.

There are risks and rewards for each kind of video, but there is no denying the potential impact of the medium. The key challenge facing online marketers is to harness this impact and take advantage of it. And yes, do not focus greatly on videos with the perfect graphics or sound either. These are definitely good to have but importantly, you have to focus on putting out information for your target audience. Once you are committed to make video part of your corporate marketing strategy, keep the faith.

## In Conclusion:
Today, most video viewers visit a video sharing site like YouTube directly or find videos through search networks. Let's rewind and refresh some tips to optimize your videos and get the most out of them.

Make sure that your videos have your branding in them. Every video should have a clear title and description as well as correct tags to identify the subject of the video.

Create a video channel and research the proper keywords to ensure that they will show up at the top of the search engine result pages. Use the channel to initiate engagement and communication with your viewers. By offering viewers the chance to rate, comment and subscribe to your videos, you will encourage interaction with your customers. Also provide the 'share' option so that it is easier for viewers to share the videos with friends. A word of caution: Avoid having videos show up on pop-up layers as these do not show up on results pages. Conduct more research to understand what the more successful videos are doing right. Check and see if those options work for you. Trial and error is the way to go!

## In the next chapter:
We shall discuss social news websites like Digg and StumbleUpon and examine strategies to market your content on these sites. We will look into ways to leverage these sites for search engine optimization and increased traffic.

# Chapter 10

## Social News

## Social News: Spread the Word

Future technology site Futurelooks wrote a story about ELP turntables with laser beams and put it up on Digg. Digg members dugg the gadget so much that it made it to the front page and in turn, brought in a flood of traffic to the Futurelooks webpage. On Digg, members vote or digg and post comments on their favorite stories or those they consider helpful or interesting. The most 'dugg' stories then appear on the front page of the website further increasing their popularity and directing more traffic towards them. Anytime you hear stories of pages getting a gazillion hits, you get excited about the possibility of your webpage or website being the recipient of so much traffic.

But how much do you know about integrating Social Media, especially social news networks, into your business promotion? Bob Buch, VP of business development for Digg, says successful Social Media integration is like chocolate chip cookies – they are made of five key ingredients. Social Media integration requires sharing, integration, people, platform and authenticity. Staying true to your core competency is important if you want to succeed on social news websites where you must catch the users' attention in an instant and retain it too.

Social News websites are communities where you can submit and share news stories, articles, videos and pictures, with the sole aim to attract traffic. These offer you a platform to showcase your content and websites to a larger audience. Today, these are powerful catalysts in viral marketing – they help circulate ideas and attract attention, traffic and links. The best thing is that you don't need to hire a PR company to promote your business. You can do it yourself! Bigger companies hire experts to help them attract traffic from these sites. UK-based news site The Telegraph implemented Smart Digg and have since then seen an incremental increase of page views on their site.

The key is to select a site that can give you long term returns on investment. The site should send prospects and traffic to your webpages while helping increase awareness about your brand or business. In this section, we will discuss StumbleUpon and Digg, which are among the most popular social news websites.

StumbleUpon allows its users to surf the Internet for relevant stories as well as to submit interesting links for the community to rate and review. Digg is a popular social news website which covers all general topics and includes a video and image section. Let's take a look at how these two social news websites operate. Just like any other marketing strategy, you will have to plan your action on these sites to exploit maximum advantage.

## StumbleUpon

StumbleUpon has over 10 million subscribers, generating up to 20 million personalized "stumbles" everyday, making it one of the most-used social bookmarking sites. It is a social networking as well as a bookmarking site with a browser toolbar that allows you to 'stumble' upon new web pages. You can tag your specific interests and the toolbar will display websites you like which you can then surf, rate, review and share with your friends. You can submit web pages to be rated by other users. The more 'thumbs up' an article receives, the more viewers it gets.

Let's look at some tips that will help you use StumbleUpon and benefit from it.

### Tips

<u>New profile</u>
Create a profile page using images, including photos or your company logo, which will appeal to your target audience. Your profile need not be your complete history but do put down information like your name, your business and any other interesting personal trivia that can set you apart from others. Use a real profile image, preferably, your own photo. Build a powerful profile by actively interacting and reviewing websites. Pay more attention to the topics of interest of your audience rather than to your own.

<u>Track favorites</u>
Track pages which get the most attention – this will help you create specific content for StumbleUpon results. One great post can drive thousands of visitors to your website!

<u>Choose smartly</u>
Stumble your best content instead of your sales page or your landing page. Space out your best pages instead of stumbling them all at once – this will drive more interaction with other members. An article on "26 Cakes Perfect for Geeks" received 290,000 stumbles!

<u>Link with Twitter, Facebook</u>
Follow StumbleUpon on your Twitter and Facebook pages and link to both sites with StumbleUpon tools to get more impact and raise traffic and brand awareness.

Be real
You must be genuine in your interactions with your StumbleUpon community. The more frequently you interact with your network, the more effective your efforts will be. Be gracious when others stumble your pages and if someone links back to you, stumble that post.

Connect with fellow bloggers
If you identify any fellow bloggers, send them a message and add them as a friend. Post your StumbleUpon profile on your blog and consistently stumble the articles of bloggers you love. This will help you connect with the blogger as well as with the readers of the blog.

**Promote your site**
Stumble Upon visitors evaluate your website with one glance and determine whether to continue browsing your site or move on to the next one. Stumblers like to see useful articles based on their interests. Do not couch advertisements in the form of content – users will see through you and thumb you down. Visitors will be attracted to valuable, interesting and unique content and good site design and will give you a lot of thumbs up and repeat visits to your website.

Your website should be visually appealing with a striking site design capable of capturing the interest of the casual surfer. Your site should offer interesting and exclusive in-depth material forcing the visitor to come back again and again. Your webpage or website should prominently feature the 'subscribe to' blog or newsletter button for alerts and updates. If there are any ads on your webpage, ensure that these are placed properly and cleanly.

Produce great content consistently – track the stories that are receiving the most stumbles and plan your content accordingly. Another way to receive repeat visitors is to conduct a contest and offer tangible benefits for winners.

**Increase traffic to your site**
Unlike search engines like Google, StumbleUpon offers much more targeted traffic. Traffic on StumbleUpon continues to flow in for a longer time for specific pages depending on content and the number of reviews it garners.

There are several factors that have an impact on the number of visitors you receive from StumbleUpon. The most important factor is the number of StumbleUpon users who give a 'thumbs up' or tag your site or page. A broad member network also adds more influence when it comes to tagging your webpage. A large number of friends also increase the authority or strength of your stumbles as most of them will not just rate but review your links as well. So connect with as many friends and with users who share your interests. Of course, a large number of reviews and thumbs up will lend you better legitimacy.

Also, while tagging keep the terms more general so there is a better chance of them being stumbled upon by the users. Web pages or sites using videos or humor retain a quarter of their traffic for a longer time. StumbleUpon is not hard to use and it would actually take you less time to promote your page here compared to other Social Media sites.

**What not to do**
StumbleUpon is a great site to find and promote great content. However, you have to be aware of the mistakes that can negatively affect marketing efforts on StumbleUpon. Let's look at some of them here.

Incomplete profile
Your profile should be complete and must have a photograph. Visitors must look forward to interacting with you and stumbling your pages, and if there is an unclear image or none at all, they will be turned off.

Sending links without comments
Write a personal thank you note to send along with the webpage link that you are sending across. Just sending links to your friends amounts to spamming and people hate spam. It is gracious to acknowledge other people's contribution to thumbing up your page.

Stumbling only your articles
It is a social site and if you spam it with your own content, people will not only stop interacting with you but you will also get banned.

Review, not just 'thumbs up'
Usually on StumbleUpon, if a page gets about 20 hits but 1 or 2 reviews, users get apprehensive about the content. Try to write as many reviews as possible.

Friend other stumblers
Add friends and if someone adds you, add them back. It increases your chances of gaining positive attention and perhaps, you can even gain partners or associates.

## Inconsistent stumbling
Be consistent in your efforts to stumble, even if it's about 8-10 stumbles every day. It lets people know that you are active. And make sure that you are discovering new articles and not just stumbling stories which have already been shown on the site to be a valuable community member.

If used correctly, StumbleUpon can direct huge traffic to your website, generate rapid exposure and a large reader base.

## Digg
Digg is quite similar to StumbleUpon. You can use this site to discover and share news stories in the form of articles, pictures or videos. Members vote or digg and post comments on their favorite stories or those that they consider helpful or interesting. The most 'dugg' stories then appear on the front page of the website further increasing their popularity and directing more traffic toward them.

Digg was one of the pioneers of social sharing on the web, even before Facebook and Twitter. Webpage publishers aimed to get on the Digg homepage and would litter their pages with 'Digg this!' buttons. If an article had enough votes to make it to the homepage, you could safely expect thousands of visitors to make a bee-line to your website within hours. Entrepreneur and Alltop founder, Guy Kawasaki got on the Digg homepage with his blog post on "The 10/20/30 Rule of PowerPoint" which drove over 10,000 visitors to his blog.

But unlike StumbleUpon, getting dugg here is a lottery. On Digg, submitted stories can be a hit or miss, whereas on StumbleUpon, every share and review can drive more interest. Digg is proving to be far less effective than sharing links with small groups of friends on networks like StumbleUpon, which enable people to share links with their friends. These friends would further encourage their friends to visit, thus steadily increasing traffic to your page.

To counteract, Digg is now offering personalized homepages to each user so that the site is more applicable to individuals and can pass on reliable traffic to webpages. Most importantly, Digg can be a great SEO tool. Digg can help websites by giving link banks and increasing popularity. But Digg's massive membership means that the competition for each entry to be one of the most dugg, is hard to attain.

## Customized experience
If your website or webpage has a Share This widget, pull the Digg and StumbleUpon

buttons from it and display these prominently. It gives your users a customized experience and helps you communicate which sites you are focused on. Conde Nast's technology news website Wired.com originally had a 'Share This' button but a closer investigation into traffic showed that most of its traffic was coming from Digg, StumbleUpon and Yahoo! Buzz. So they removed these sites from under Share This! and placed them separately on the pages. This time, the Digg traffic rose from 500,000 clicks to over a million.

Here are some tips to help you use Digg to your website's advantage and leverage it to attract traffic to your web pages.

## Dig these tips

### Profile
Your username should either complement the image and purpose of your website or advertise your expertise in a particular field.

### Submit stories
Make sure that your stories are unique and have catchy titles and descriptions. Do not put up old news – submit fresh news. Better still, put up stories that provide helpful information to users - such stories will interest your readers and raise its sharing possibility. Be witty and creative - your stories should be worth the reader's time.

### Title and summary
Make sure that your stories have a great title and summary to interest the readers to check out your site. These are your tools to convince other users to click on the submission, read the article and Digg it.

### Add friends
Add friends based on the basis of a few key factors. Find out members who digg a lot, submit stories very often or have lots of friends. In Digg, you can view updates of your friends' network, so if you have a new entry, there is a good chance that all the friends of your friend can view it. Do not add friends too fast! Digg might figure you are a 'bot'. Be sure to pace it out.

### Digg friends' stories
You want others to Digg your stories, so begin by digging the stories of your friends. When you digg someone's story, they notice your profile which in turn, offers them a chance to view and digg your stories. Register with Digg Alerts to receive alerts

whenever any of your friends have posted on Digg.

## Digg good stories
On Digg, find good quality stories quickly and digg as much as possible. Avoid digging stories that seem to have interesting titles but have no valuable content.

## Comment on rising stories
Search for stories that you think can become very popular in the community and comment on them. Remember to leave links to your website and related sites. This will give you a chance to have your comment at the top comments page. Other members will be curious to open your profile. Of course, your comment must add some valuable information for the community and your links must be relevant to the discussion. Please do not spam – you will get banned.

## Active Digger
By being an active Digg user, you have a better chance at attracting Diggs to your submissions from other users. The more active you are, more people will notice you and will be interested in checking out your submissions, creating more opportunities for a Digg. More Diggs for your posts will result in more traffic to your webpage.

## Ask for a digg
If you really need diggs on a particular story and you think it is interesting, you can politely ask the community or the top Diggers to vote for your story. Do not be turned off or be provoked by any rude comments. And add Digg This! button in your blog posts, webpages, and RSS feeds.

**Difference between Digg & StumbleUpon**
Digg has a larger prevalence of tech-savvy users, probably because it has become a niche for technology enthusiasts though other categories perform well too. StumbleUpon tends to have a heterogeneous user base, even though it has its share of tech-savvy members. News stories tend to do slightly better on Digg while videos, guides and humor fare slightly better on StumbleUpon.

Another key difference is in the way both sites function. Digg has a section showcasing new stories that users can vote up or down. But with thousands of entries being submitted every day, you cannot expect to get enough traffic from this alone. Visibility on Digg depends on how much traction your stories get. If your content can become popular and make the front page, Digg will send loads of traffic your way. Sites have reported receiving over 100,000 visits in a single day. However, if it doesn't, your content will be among the many thousands that do not get enough visibility or traffic.

On StumbleUpon, the toolbar allows its users to scroll up and down and vote the webpages of their interest. The more 'thumbs up' a story gets, the more people view it through the Stumble toolbar as it will get voted up driving traffic to your page. So even if you do not experience traffic spikes to your webpage, you will see at least some amount of traffic. Also, StumbleUpon offers gradual traffic that lasts for a long time.

Also, StumbleUpon lets you categorize your submissions into selective fields like entrepreneurship, surfing etc. while Digg offers more generic categories making it difficult to find entries on specific topics.
However, in general, both are very good social bookmarking sites and can help increase website traffic and promote awareness about your business.

These are based on our observations about the two Social Media sites. However, irrespective of the site you select, you will have to work to create a brand presence. If you can prove yourself as being quite helpful to the community, the members will steadily recognize your efforts and you can rely on them to send traffic to your webpages. It is important to follow the web community etiquettes on both sites while communicating with members. Always be ready to acknowledge and thank the reader who originally spread the word about your story.

If your story has made it to the Digg homepage, find the reader who championed your story. You will find their profile picture (avatar) right below your story. You can befriend them and even send them a personal note, if an email id is published on their profile. On StumbleUpon, find your story and click the white speech bubble in the toolbar. You will see the first reader to stumble your story on the upper right hand side (in a blue box). Click on their avatar and use the 'send message' button to convey your thanks and add them as a friend.

Enjoy digging and stumbling!

**In the next chapter:**
We will discuss some more Social Media sites like Flickr, Yahoo! Answers, SlideShare and Yelp. We will take a look at how to get noticed on Flickr and how to market your business on Flickr. We will also examine ways to use the other sites to better promote your business.

# Chapter 11

# Best of the Rest
# (Yahoo, Flickr, etc.)

# Best of the Rest

Social Media is all about spreading and sharing a buzz. But for companies to benefit from it, they need to have a sound and practical strategy in place. Look at how a ubiquitous baby products company has managed to build a community around their products using Flickr. Graco's blog promotes its Flickr stream that showcases cute pictures of babies, prompting other users to follow suit. It also posts pictures from its community gatherings to the Flickr stream, thus combining offline and online marketing efforts to build a loyal audience base. The point is: Though most often Social Media marketing discussions revolve around the usual suspects like YouTube, Facebook, Twitter and LinkedIn, there are several other Social Media platforms you can use with great effect to market your company or brand. Let's look at some of them.

## Flickr

Here is a real-life incident that illustrates the Flickr power! A visual arts student in Iceland, Rebekka Guðleifsdóttir, began posting stark, evocative photographs on Flickr. Soon the budding photographer gained a good following among the site's users. One of them, working in Toyota's marketing department, contacted Rebekka to check whether she was interested in an ad campaign for their hybrid model. Soon she was shooting official posters for the company. Her success story aptly sums up the spirit of Social Media.

## Features of Flickr

Images can be very narrative. People prefer to glance at them rather than simply scrolling down those elaborate descriptions. After all, as they rightly say, "a picture is worth a thousand words." This is especially true when you take into account the very short attention span of virtual visitors.

With its massive size and active user base, Flickr has emerged as one of the most popular photo-sharing sites. Starting out as a community for photography professionals and hobbyists, it now lets generic users with diverse interests upload photos - personal or professional – of family affairs, celebrations, events, company products and services. The vast Flickr community can easily view them. Sometimes, there is a potential risk of losing all your precious photos on a third party site if it fails. Flickr is extremely reliable on this count.

With Yahoo! acquiring it in 2005, Flickr was optimized with the Yahoo! Image Search tool. This means when one uses Yahoo! to search for images on specific topics, Flickr pictures will be displayed. For a corporate blog, Flickr is a great way to showcase pictures. You can upload your pictures and save on bandwidth. Also, Flickr can help build traffic to your site. The photos get listed in Google, Technorati, Ask.com and other portals. Websites and blogs pull in and display Flickr pictures through RSS feeds. All these sources can be funneled back to your own site, to enlighten the prospective customers about your brand, products or services.

**Steps to set up your account**
To get started on Flickr, you first need to sign up. You can log in and edit your settings by filling in the requisite information. You can create your profile by adding a buddy icon, screen name, relevant links and data about yourself or your business.

Screen name
Make your website URL the same as your screen name. Because your screen name will be attached to everything you do on Flickr – uploaded photos, discussions, messages etc. You could also use the name of your brand.

Profile
You can use your profile to advertise your company. It is your platform to sell yourself and lure attention. Take advantage of it. Describe yourself and your business, your location and your interests to personalize your profile. Include relevant links like your website name and address. Avoid making any sales pitches in the profile.

Buddy icon
You can also upload a 'Buddy Icon' in the profile. Its size is small (48x48 pixels) so make sure to upload a visually appealing and noticeable avatar. Ideally, use your company logo or brand image.

Flickr address
Create your own Flickr address to easily share your pictures with others. For example: www.flickr.com/photos/heavenly-cupcakes

**Free versuspaid account**
You can sign up for either a free or paid version. The free version will allow you a bandwidth limit of 100MB each month (10MB per photo), which is ideal if you do not have too much traffic or have limited size photos. You can make 2 video uploads each month, photostream views will be limited to the 200 most recent images and you can post any of your photos in up to 10 group pools. However, the paid version (Pro Account) allows you unlimited bandwidth, and you can make nearly unlimited photo and video uploads. You can set up an unlimited number of photo sets, archive

high-resolution original images, replace a photo, and post any of your photos or videos in up to 60 group pools. All this comes at a nominal annual payment!

**Uploading and tagging pictures**
To easily upload pictures, use the Flickr Web interface or other uploading tools like Flickr's desktop program that uploads and tags images really quickly. Tag your pictures with the relevant keywords so that the top search engines, as well as other Flickr users, can easily find them. There are three main elements to consider while tagging a picture (You can also add a watermark of your website link on your photos!).

Title
Use descriptive, but relevant, titles and keywords for the title. Be careful that the title does not become too long.

Tags
Tags can be seen on the right side bar of each photo. Add relevant 'tags' or keywords that should describe each photo you upload. Add location tags if your business targets a specific local region. Do not stuff irrelevant tags into your images in search of a hit. Your tags must represent your image.

Description
Give proper and accurate descriptions to each photo. The quality of the photos must be the priority rather than your sales pitch. Links with descriptive titles get better click through rates. You can use HTML in the picture description. If the picture is used in a specific Webpage, add a link to it. If not, put a general link to your website. Remember to use attractive anchor text.

**Tips to market your business on Flickr**
It is very easy to use Flickr to promote your business. Let's consider some vital pointers that will help you to implement your marketing plan.

- Take and upload good quality photos of your products/services or anything related to your business. For example, if you are a caterer, upload photos of your events - your staff, food, overall presentation etc. The Internet products company, Directi, uses Flickr to post pictures of office events, outings, meetings as well as candid photos to convey the fun atmosphere prevailing in their offices. Such photo sets can be a great asset for start-ups and small companies toward recruiting top-notch talent.

- Join and share your photos in appropriate groups. Flickr has plenty of groups for just about anything. Do you make homemade candles or customized handbags? You will find several groups for you to join. You can also join location specific groups related to your city or state. Posting photos and participating in discussions in these groups will help you reach a local audience.

- Avoid adding your photo to all sundry groups. You should ideally add a photo to five or six groups at first, then remove it from a few of them and post it to some others. This will allow you to see your photo on the front page of many groups!

- Link to your Flickr account from your website. This is important as people visiting your website may well be interested in your photos. Those active on Flickr are most likely to add you to their list of contacts. On your part, remember to return the favor! Also, search engine crawlers can follow a prominent link from your site to your Flickr photos, which will give you more potential matches for search engine users.

- Flickr is about building a community. Interact with other people if you want them to visit your account. Add good photos to your Favorites and comment on photos you like, even if they are not related to your business. Uploading good photos and commenting on other people's pictures will give you more visibility. Participate in key group discussions. Each activity will display your screen name and if you have used your URL as your screen name, that's a bonus promotion.

- Organize your photos. Create sets. Add relevant photos to them. Remove irrelevant images from them. This helps your visitors have a pleasant and clutter-free experience. Avoid posting too many similar-looking photos. Select the best images in a series and display them. Remember, a good viewing experience is more about quality than quantity!

- You can also use Flickr to search photos related to your business and products uploaded by other users. Perhaps, your customers have already uploaded photos about your products/services. You can monitor customer feedback and respond to it. Do not spam other users' photos with self-promotional messages. Avoid using linked keywords in your photo descriptions or in your comments. Flickr users do not look kindly at such behavior.

If you can follow these steps, you will be on your way to a more fruitful experience on Flickr. As with any other promotional strategy, you have to devote enough time to take care of all the small details that ultimately make a difference.

## Yahoo! Answers

Early on in his campaign in 2007, Barack Obama asked a question: "How can we engage more people in the democratic process?" It is a question often posed by politicians. But what was new was the platform he used to pose it. He was neither talking to any reporter nor was he addressing a gathering. He had opted for Yahoo! Answers to reach out to its countless users in one go. Within a week, he had received about 15,000 answers.

Now you know why Yahoo! Answers is considered among the most popular reference sites on the Web, just behind Wikipedia. Yahoo! Answers is a social network focused on knowledge sharing based on a questions-and-answers format. In this online community, you can ask questions on any topic and receive a variety of responses from real people. In a minute, there are dozens of questions asked by users and during peak times, there could be over 100 questions posed. Launched by Yahoo! in 2005, the service surpassed the market share of the now-defunct Google Answers within the first two months (according to Hitwise).

Yahoo! Answers applies a point system that does not offer any real time rewards except for status privileges. If you have moved up a level, you get additional privileges like asking and answering more questions, rating other questions, etc. You earn points by answering questions and then by getting your answer judged 'Best Answer' or getting a 'thumbs up' from other users. Interestingly, you lose points by asking a question – this is to keep the quality of questions high.

On Yahoo! Answers, you will come across many professionals and business owners willing to provide valuable knowledge and to share their experiences. When you give great answers, you are able to build credibility for yourself and to create a positive brand image. If your answer is precise and on-topic, you can add a link to your website, blog, or email to offer more relevant information. But do not look at it as a sales pitch. You can use it as a promotional tool only within the implicit norms.

### How to use Yahoo! Answers

<u>Profile page</u>
Your profile page tracks your activities, including every question asked, answered or rated, as well as any points earned while using the service. You can add links in your profile but it is 'nofollowed' meaning you cannot link to the page from your profile. You can add friends, invite friends to join the service, and vote on other answers. Build your friend network carefully, because your friends' questions are highlighted on your profile and it is best to have high quality questions in your profile.

## Use RSS feeds

On Yahoo! Answers, every category in the system has its own RSS feed. When looking for available questions to answer, find the categories you want to follow and subscribe to the RSS feed. For example, if you are an expert on food, you could go to Dining Out or the Food and Drink category and look for the RSS link. And if you are unable to find suitable categories, use the search box to find questions that you would like to answer. A note of caution: Sometimes the RSS feeds may be delayed and it is best to visit the site and search for questions to answer.

## Use sorting

Once you have reached a category, the page will have the most recent questions. Additionally, you could also use the sorting options to look for questions. You can either sort by date or by the number of answers.

**By date:** One easy way is to sort for questions that are about to expire. Each question is open for four days and users can extend a question once by another four days. If these questions have no answers, or very few answers, you can write the best answer to get an easy 10 points. This option helps build your points profile but doesn't do much for visibility.

**By answers:** This can help boost your exposure and branding. Search for questions that are receiving a lot of answers, then write a great answer and add your link, if appropriate. This will give you a chance to be seen by a lot of people and direct some traffic to your site or blog.

## Leave your name

When you are answering a question, make sure to leave your name as it distinguishes you from spammers. In online communities, only spammers do not leave their names because often, they would just drop links in the answers. Folks, leave your link only when answering relevant topics. And no spam, please! Use your discretion and common sense while adding links to your website, blogs or contact information with your answers. Refer to the guidelines if you are not sure.

### Traffic from Yahoo! Answers

If your business is specifically about knowledge and expertise, Yahoo! Answers is an excellent sales tool. By providing useful answers, you can brand yourself and attract new traffic to your website. Keep aside some time during the week or even daily, if your schedule permits, and search for questions to answer. You can also subscribe to select category RSS feeds for questions. Yahoo! Answers can be a great source of referral traffic. It is also an indirect source of search engine traffic and Yahoo! Answers pages show up on search engine result pages. So you can get traffic from Google, Yahoo! or MSN.

If used correctly, Yahoo! Answers can form an important tool in your overall sales strategy. It can provide small businesses and entrepreneurs with an opportunity to gain exposure, improve branding, and acquire loyal customers. A successful business model is built more on trust and relationships than anything else. With Yahoo! Answers, small businesses can establish trust by responding to potential customers' queries. Of course, like any other social site, focus on what you can give to the community.

**Yelp**
Yelp is a business review site, which has built a reputation for honest appraisal of the quality of services like restaurants, bars, bookstores, accountants, and realtors among others. People in urban centers often check it for suggestions and reviews on places to dine, to purchase bags or to be entertained.

Blogger Michael Lynton has shared his experience of finding a home mortgage service through Yelp. On the verge of buying a house, he and his wife locked in a previous mortgage provider for the new house. However, soon they learned that the house would not be ready in time and his locked-in rate would expire around the same time. The provider informed Lynton that he would have to pay a fee to extend the period. Dissatisfied with the deal, he went public on Yelp and soon found a lender, who offered a lower rate than before and crowned it with great local service.

So if you are a local small business, list yourself on Yelp. If you can use the platform correctly, you can bring in new business and prevent negative feedback from affecting your business growth. To begin with, create your Yelp business page by filling out an online form and answering a quick, automated phone call. Once signed up, you can use the available tools to engage your customers and promote your services to the community.

Here we share with you a few basic tips to leverage Yelp to benefit your business:

- Customers refer to Yelp business pages to learn more about a business before visiting in person. If the information on your Yelp page is incomplete, they could move on to a competitor that provides more details. The page for business owners offers options to share vital information to make it easy for users to know what to expect from you. Providing more details about your business will help potential customers to know your services better, multiplying your chances of them turning into reliable customers. So ensure that you fill out as much information as possible and keep it updated.

- Yelp enables business owners to respond to negative reviews by either privately apologizing or by publicly correcting misinformation. If your business has received negative comments, do not take it personally. Customers would like you to communicate with them and they will give you a second chance if you can convey that you are using their valuable input to improve your business. You can look up Yelp's guide to constructive user review responses too.

- On Yelp, you can introduce special offers for visitors to your page and it will get largely viewed, as it appears in the offers and announcements directory for your city! This will not only make your business visible to people, but it will also show your business in search results. Use creative ways to promote your business and to attract people.

- You can embed Yelp badges on your business website or blog to show that you are engaged with the Yelp community. Your badges display the number of positive reviews you have received letting potential customers know that your customers are satisfied and hence, you are trustworthy. Clicking on a badge will take a visitor to read reviews or more information. It may even encourage the satisfied customers to leave their own positive review.

- If you have great customer service, the people will come. Yelp will help you attract new customers and these people will be more likely to share their review on Yelp.

**SlideShare**
SlideShare is an online slide hosting service, which lets you upload, favorites, bookmark, tag, and comment on slide show presentations online. It also allows users to discover relevant content and connect with other members with similar interests. You can upload files in PowerPoint, PDF, or OpenOffice presentation formats.

The San Francisco based company has seen a rapid growth in traffic since its launch in 2006, mostly from companies and organizations. Users call the sharing site the 'YouTube for presentations.' Businesses use it to network with each other and share their content on the basis of their intellectual property ranging from documents, white papers, to Webinars and presentations. Recognizing the role of businesses and entrepreneurs in its success, it regularly rolls out new and compelling services to business users.

## How to use it?
You can use slide shows to deliver all sorts of content. You can create 'how to' tutorials, make a sales presentation, present case studies creatively, bring existing presentations online and explain complex business processes through visual aids. Use big visuals and fewer words - create lots of white space - to attract more views to your SlideShare presentations. You can join groups, download slideshows, and receive codes to embed or link to slideshows on your website or blog. Become an active networker on SlideShare. Comment, list your favorites, join groups, and link to slideshows to boost your slideshow's visibility.

## Important features
SlideShare offers branded channels, which help users to find this content easily and in a more organized manner. Even the White House has created branded channels on SlideShare. You can fully customize your branded channels. Pricing varies depending on the business' preferred layout.

LeadShare is a self-service tool that businesses can use to capture leads through your content like documents and presentations. Most whitepaper campaigns require users to fill out information to get the whitepaper. It enables you to embed a presentation onto a site and allows users to view and download it before filling out a contact form. LeadShare only charges for leads generated so you only pay for users who actually want more information, rather than for everyone who views your presentations. You can also use it to specify the kind of information you want to capture to target your most probable audience. LeadShare's method can help aid businesses trying to target specific customers.

On the other hand, AdShare allows businesses to promote their own content via ads on the SlideShare platform. Businesses can now promote their content alongside other relevant content. AdShare lets you monitor the effectiveness of your content as content gets displayed based on the number of clicks received by each content type.

Users can access SlideShare on their mobile by pointing your mobile phone browser to m.slideshare.com. If you have any smart phone or a phone with Opera Mini installed, you can browse for the latest and popular presentations. SlideShare supports embedded audio alongside slideshows. Users can also embed YouTube videos into their Flash-based presentations on SlideShare. The videos can be a personal introduction to the slideshow, additional content for the presentation, or demonstrations of a website's features.

# Optimizing with SlideShare

## Keywords in title, summary
The slideshow title is the title tag of the page. You are allowed fewer words on the page so your title must successfully convey the subject and purpose of the slideshow. The slide summary should be brief and informative. Sprinkle relevant keywords within the summary. This will make it easier for visitors and search engines.

## Tags
You can use tags on your slideshows to help users find your content while searching for various topics. You can also tag links in case users want to go to the full article on the site.

## Larger text in slides
Use larger text in the slides so that they are readable because the slide show will be much smaller once published on SlideShare. Remember the slides will look larger on your computer screen so do not judge readability based on how it looks on the screen. Of course, users can download the slideshow but you do not want them to skip your presentation because they are unable to read it in the smaller format.

Once the content is published on SlideShare, search engines are able to index them fairly quickly. You can use SlideShare to drive direct and measurable business results. Social Media is about the power of collaboration. So go ahead and share your expertise on SlideShare and establish your unique branding.

**In conclusion:**
By being a smart and active contributor to Social Media sites, your business can derive precious indirect marketing exposure. The more active you are in the community, the more exposure your profile will gain, thus increasing traffic to your site.

There is no doubt that Social Media can help create a buzz about your website through pictures. If used properly, it can serve as an effective marketing tool for small businesses. The key is to respect the community and be an active and responsible member, and avoid using sales tactics in your photos and posts.

**In the next chapter:**
We will discuss search engine optimization techniques and understand how Social Media has changed the search engine interface. We will also look into Social Media strategies for SEO as well as a list of SEO-friendly Social Media sites.

# Chapter 12

# Social Media and Search Engine Optimization

# Social Media & Search Engine Optimization

Georgia-based Metro Wheels owns a wheel/rim repair facility and also sells new and used alloy wheels across the southeastern United States. In 2005, the company decided to use its website to generate leads and approached an internet marketing agency to help them with search engine optimization. The goal was to attain top ranking in search engine results for keywords like "alloy wheels," "wheel repair," and "rim repair." As these are some of the most competitive auto industry search terms, the agency simultaneously targeted the less competitive keywords to get quick rankings and boost traffic to the site. For link building, the agency listed the website in web directories, exchanged links, published articles online and set up an RSS feed. Part of the campaign also included amending keywords, writing keyword-rich copy, enhancing navigation, adding fresh content and continuing the link building process. Within 5 months, Metro Wheels was featured on the first page of Google for these competitive keywords.

### Search Engine Optimization
Search Engine Optimization (SEO) is the definition for various techniques to optimize web pages or websites to make them more visible in search engines and get excellent rankings in search result pages. Optimizing a website may involve editing its content and HTML text, editing its associated coding and increasing inbound links to increase its relevance to specific keywords. Keywords help search engines in their indexing activities. The ultimate goal of SEO is to drive targeted traffic to your site.

In 2007, search engine giant Google announced a critical change in the way it showed search results to its users. With the introduction of Universal Search, businesses had to optimize not only their website text, but also other content like images and videos. Google's step is a pointer to the search engine's recognition of the growing importance and popularity of Social Media.

Prior to this, search engine result pages only displayed text links. If you wanted images, you had to go to the images tab and then conduct a search. Increasingly, search engines like Google and Bing are showing up universal search results. Google, Ask, Yahoo and MSN are among the pioneers of universal search.

So search engines are now incorporating Social Media into their search results. Social Media marketing is increasingly an integral part of online marketing strategies as it can drive huge volumes of traffic and links to sites; these have a direct influence on search engine rankings. Social Media marketing can rank not only your websites but also your pictures, videos, blogs or press releases on the first page of Google. To sustain your rankings on Google's front page, you need a consistent strategy. A good Social Media campaign can get your website a lot of viral links which are critical to an effective SEO campaign.

With blended results, search engines integrate images, websites, videos, local maps, book listings, news and even real time Social Media links like blogs and tweets into general search results. For example, if you conduct a Google search for The Rolling Stones, you will get text results like news stories or website links as well as links to videos and images. The various types of blended search results include: Images, Videos, Blogs, Book Listings, PDFs, Local Search Listings, Text Links as well as product searches, job searches, people searches and map searches.

## Blended Search

Google says, "The ultimate goal of universal search is to break down the silos of information that exist on the web and provide the very best answer every time a user enters a query."

Blended search (or universal search) is a new opportunity for marketers. You can now optimize your content to appear in blended search results on search engines. Though blended search has been around for a while, B2B marketers haven't exactly caught on to its importance. For marketers this is an interesting development. After all, if a potential customer has a question, it pays to provide search engines with your 'very best answer.'

## Why should you optimize for blended search?

Optimizing for universal/blended search must be one of the main areas of focus becauseit is critical for your online marketing strategy. For example, what if your website has enjoyed high page ranks on key search terms with a search engine for years but now you find that these pages have been pushed down the rankings by video, image or other types of blended search results? This happens because blended search looks for relevancy based on the search query. So search engines will show the most relevant results irrespective of whether it is a video or a podcast.

Simple text link results are being replaced by dynamic and more targeted search results. So how do you optimize for blended search?

## Optimize existing content

Begin by optimizing your existing website content for the search engines. Especially, page titles, metadata and page copy. Even if text link search results are one among many dynamic results, these are still an important part of the search page. Optimizing content holds the key because otherwise useful social content like blogs, videos, images and audio will not be discovered through search. For example, there have been various instances of companies optimizing their 'About us' page on their website using recommended keywords. Add other on page elements like back links which are links from other sites that point to your site. Importantly, get back links from websites that have relevant content to your site. In one particular case, a month after optimizing the 'About Us' page, the website witnessed a 26% increase in visitors from Google and over a 40% rise in visitors from Yahoo! And the icing on the cake was that the main keyword in the page saw over 1500% increase in visitor traffic.

**Optimize images**
Optimizing images is a key factor that is commonly overlooked. Address this issue by providing descriptive and keyword-rich alt text to all images. Optimize images for size. Use proper naming conventions for images – optimize the images on your site for your key phrases. For example, instead of Image1.jpg, it should be publishingkeynote.jpg

**Organize your content**
Review your existing content and find out if certain content can be served to your users in various formats. To name a few, content can be presented as videos, video transcripts, blog content, press release news content and PDFs.

Optimize and upload videos
With search engines incorporating more video results into their search results, it is even more important to optimize and upload your videos for your users. If you are releasing a new product - upload a video to promote it. Each video must have its own metadata. Metadata explains the video's content and should be descriptive and keyword rich. Most video results tend to be from external video aggregator sites like YouTube, so make sure to post your videos on these sites.

Optimize press releases
Optimize news releases similar to a standard web page by using keywords often and linking to relevant content. Syndicate company news through RSS feeds and press releases – This will ensure better chances of news /press releases about your company showing up in the blended search results.

## Add fresh content regularly
Always add fresh content to your web pages whether it's page content, white papers or new images, videos or podcasts. Fresh content can help you promote various forms of your content for blended search. Blended search results factor in relevancy and give more weight to fresh content in the search results.

## Blog regularly
Blogs are amongst the more trusted form of web content. And search engines are incorporating more blog content into their main results. Blogging can get your content quickly onto the web and can get ranked in the search engines within hours. Also, starting a blog can help you communicate with the online community. Blogs can go a long way in establishing an online reputation or reviving a sagging reputation by clarifying issues in a blog post.

Look beyond just text on your web pages. Internet users continue to prefer interactive content forms. Optimizing all images, videos, news releases and all other existing content by tagging might seem daunting but it will be worth the investment. Blended search optimization of your web properties should be part of your long-term online marketing strategy. Or else, you must be prepared to face drops in search page rankings. This will cost you more in the end. So take control of search results.

## **Social Media Strategies for SEO**
There is immense pressure on marketers to improve performance by using fewer resources and digital measures like search engine optimization and Social Media. The link between Social Media and search is evolving with engines and the social web innovating and integrating each other to make both more valuable to the users. Linking search engine optimization with Social Media marketing tactics can offer increased social network discovery through search as well as attract links for better SEO.

Until now, if your link performed well enough to feature on the front page of Digg, StumbleUpon or other such social news sites, you could get a large volume of links to your webpage. But now you can also use Social Media sites like Twitter or Facebook to network and share information. Search engines consider links shared on these popular Social Media platforms as high quality links and ranks them higher on the search results. Many companies use Social Media as a PR mechanism for promotion and share links to their web pages.

A major factor is that search engines trust a link from a highly trusted website. So if your webpage gets several mentions across Social Media sites, the search engine will take this as a strong ranking signal. There is another reason why search engines may consider Social Media as ranking signals. It is difficult to run a spam campaign on Social Media as you will get exposed quite soon.

As a marketer, if you can integrate Social Media into your PR strategy, you will not only see positive market exposure but also much improved search engine rankings. For an effective Social Media strategy for SEO, you have to identify your target audience and your goals and objectives.

## Identify your audience
The key is to understand the behavior, preferences and the methods of sharing practiced by your target audience. Companies have to invest in finding channels where their target audience spends its time interacting and sharing content. Companies who have been on Social Media sites track their audience through Social Media monitoring software that identifies keywords within conversations.

## Define goals
SEO in Social Media mainly exists to influence target audiences to discover social content or groups through search. Social content can increase visits to your website, improve traffic and influence online sales. When a user runs a search, search engines should throw up all relevant content in diverse channels like Twitter, Digg or YouTube.

**Establish strategy**
Based on your findings, you have to decide whether regularly publishing new keyword-rich content or creating user-generated interactive content will help you reach your goals. Whichever strategy you decide upon, you must actively promote relevant web pages and encourage sharing them with the rest of the community.

Social Media can affect your SEO efforts both positively and negatively. Marketers have to learn to complement Social Media with SEO. Let us see how Social Media marketing can directly impact search engine listings.

## Place website links on Social Media sites
Social Media websites like Facebook and Twitter are very influential in the search engines. Most Social Media websites are invaluable for powerful links and top-ranked search influence. To begin, place your website link on major Social Media profiles like Facebook and Twitter pages. Every link placed on your social profiles is a potential PR boost. Remember, use keyword rich content to see your site succeed on Social Media platforms and search engines.

### Fresh, updated content
The more content you add to your site, the better your chances to increase traffic to your site. Fresh content keeps your site updated and gives your readers a reason to keep coming back. Also search engines like updated sites. Thus, fresh content will bring in frequent visits through searches. If you continue to update your site with fresh content, search engines will begin to index your pages hours after publishing.

### Compelling content wins
Unique and compelling content is the fulcrum on which your Social Media strategy spins. Without it, nothing matters. Social Media users often link to the best content and search engines, and Social Media users rank unique content on top.

### Quality inbound links
If you have a successful Social Media marketing campaign, it can attract thousands of new inbound links to your site. Inbound links are an important factor in influencing your site's ranking. Some brands and companies have managed to sell their products through Social Media campaigns. But most marketers focus on building their online reputation using Social Media sites so that at the time of product launch, they can leverage that influence into sales. Even a single article promoted across various Social Media networks can result in mass link building and huge SEO influence.

### Reputation management
The more popular Social Media sites rank well within the search engines. So anything positive or negative about your company or brand will be easily visible to anyone searching for your company. You can leverage Social Media sites by sharing links about your company or web page on Digg, Twitter or YouTube. This will help you show up on the first page of search results for your name or site and help build your digital reputation, which in turn, will result in increased traffic and links.

You can also monitor search results to check if there are negative comments about your brand or product. By checking regularly, you can identify complaints and issue clarifications to address issues.

### Showcase webpages on Social Media sites
If your new site is not showing up on search engine results pages, showcase your site on a Social Media site. Search engines trust Social Media sites and rank them extremely well on results pages. For example, upload some videos on YouTube or begin a blog and build some good links to it. Initially, Social Media sites will direct traffic to your pages but soon, direct traffic will stream in for your unique content.

## Social Media is sustainable

Initially, you have to build a community based on honest and fresh content. You must share your unique ideas and opinions with members of your community. Encourage members to initiate and conduct discussions. These discussions and debates could inspire new ideas from you.

## Social Media users share

Social Media users are savvy enough to share your content with the rest of the web. If your link has been blogged or Dugg by influential bloggers or Diggers, the rest of community will most likely share that link with their 'friends.'

For small businesses, Social Media sites and search engine optimization can direct traffic to your website. Any mention of your link on a Social Media forum becomes an inbound link that sends visitors to your website. Blogs, tweets and social news sites can help you monitor your Social Media efforts. For optimization, highlighting specific keywords is a must.

Ken Savage's blogging story can be an inspiration. After being diagnosed with Type 2 Diabetes, Ken made an effort to learn more about the disease. With a desire to share information about diabetes research with others, Ken launched his BattleDiabetes.com blog. Ken's search engine friendly blog attracts close to 10,000 page views daily with most of the traffic coming from search engines like Google and Ask.com. He has also listed his blog in major niche web directories like Aviva Directory and Business.com. He also links his blog posts on social news sites like StumbleUpon and Digg to build some of his traffic. All this has resulted in an increase in search driven traffic. Ken has combined his passion, SEO and link building along with advertising to turn the diagnosis of a life threatening disease into a commercial opportunity as well as a social service by preventing others from developing his disease.

## Social Media measures at a glace

Let's summarize Social Media measures that small marketers can use for SEO.

### Blogs
- Create a company blog and leverage blog posts to create links of web pages from your website. Use relevant and keyword-rich anchor text.
- Share blog posts with fellow bloggers and other influencers. Focus on unique content to get their attention.
- Get influential bloggers to write on your blog or conduct an interview with them

and share the link on your site as well as on theirs. That particular blogger's fans will bring in additional traffic and if you have compelling content, some of them will return.

Twitter
- Use Twitter to engage with bloggers and other influencers.
- Follow them on Twitter, @ reply them sometimes and retweet their content. Establish engagement with them before sending them a link.

Social news
- Create a profile on popular social bookmarking sites like Digg and StumbleUpon to build and promote engagement. These sites can help your content go viral resulting in hundreds of inbound links impacting SEO and incoming traffic to your site.
- Point to note: Unique content is a must for this to work.

Micro sites and Social channels
- Create micro sites for specific Social Media campaigns. Be sure to optimize it for search. Keywords and metadata are the cornerstones to an effective SEO strategy which can deliver thousands or even millions of visitors to the site.
- Create a presence on sites such as blogs, YouTube, Facebook, Twitter and optimize them. These Social Media channels help in reputation management and branding.

**In conclusion:**
Search engine optimization and search engine marketing are increasingly overlapping each other. Search strategies require similar marketing skills and customer insight to boost brand awareness, drive registrations or increase sales. Accept this change. More visibility will bring additional interaction with your brand.

**In the next chapter:**
You will be introduced to Online Reputation Management where we willdiscuss ways to monitor and manage poor and unfavourable search engine and social media posts. We will also explain strategies to ensure that you are never caught offgaurd, which can hurt your brand and make your business suffer.

## Chapter 13

# Social Media and Online Reputation Management

# Social Media and Online Reputation Monitoring and Management

In 2005, Jeff Jarvis frustrated with his Dell laptop and customer service experience wrote a blog post titled "Dell sucks." Within days, thousands of frustrated people had commented on and linked to his blog saying "I agree." The story was covered by analysts and journalists and Dell had to try hard to fight the damage to their company image. Jarvis even wrote an open letter to Michael Dell suggesting that his company should read blogs, ask customers for opinions as well as write blogs to "join the conversation your customers are having without you." Within a year, Dell launched its Direct2Dell blog to deal with customer issues. Dell also launched IdeaStorm.com where customers can write in their suggestions to the company. Now the company even allows customers to rate its products on its site.

If you own a company or organization, brand monitoring is essential. In today's well-connected world, we only need to type selected keywords into search engines to get a comprehensive view of the conversations discussing us, our brands and our companies. Conversations on the web happen with or without our consent. Web conversations around your brand could be either user generated content or a journalistic piece. These can define the brand's image for existing and potential customers. Negative reviews of your products will result in falling sales and a devalued brand.

You have the choice to observe or participate, as and when required or to overlook them completely. Point to note though -- conversations on the web travel like wild fire and if negative in nature, they can cause immense damage to your brand. Keeping updated with people's reactions and feedback about your products is the key to understanding your customers' requirements. In case of complaints from customers, brand monitoring helps entrepreneurs and companies to provide appropriate rebuttals or clarifications. On the other hand, positive reviews in the Social Media world can stimulate great benefits.

The goal is good public relations. Ask Domino's Pizza about the YouTube video posted by two stupid employees. In the video, the employees play with various food products - like inserting cheese into their nose – before placing them on orders. A single three-minute video was enough to unravel the brand image that Domino's had built up assiduously over the years. Within a day, the video had over 720,000 hits and Dominos had thousands of outraged patrons. An awareness of Social Media and ways it can be utilized to make or damage a brand could have saved the company many headaches and Public Relations scrambling. Ignore Social Media at your peril!

Monitoring certain keywords crucial to your business, across the Web in search blogs, forums, news, is online reputation monitoring. Any measures you take to tackle negative online publicity will be part of your Online Reputation Management. Social Media is changing the Public Relations (PR) blueprint and therefore, plays a major crucial role in "managing" your online reputation.

Social Media monitoring acquired prominence as companies started realizing the power of Social Media to influence consumer behavior. The increasing amount of user generated content on the web made it easier for consumers to build opinions about companies and brands based on the search results. Consequently, companies began participating in Social Media networks in a bid to influence their consumers.

**Strategies for online brand monitoring**

Ear to the ground er…the Web
To monitor your brand, you have to listen to what people are saying about you in various places like Twitter, blogs and other social networks. Keeping track of their conversations can help you to respond accordingly. By listening, you can better position your company in your niche industry as well as adapt effectively to the changing economy. You have to take the initiative to listen. Prepare a personal branding strategy based on your requirements. There are several tools like Twitter search and Google alerts, among others which make it easier to track online discussions and mentions about you. Take advantage of these tools and stay ahead of your competition.

The key to landing clients through Social Media is to build relationships with the right audience. Jon Phillips of Montreal-based Spyre Studios has used an active Twitter presence to connect with small business owners, freelancers, designers and developers. Jon says that several bloggers have included him in 'Tweeple to follow if you are into…' lists which act as a recommendation from these people.

Build a company website
Anytime someone searches for you, your company or your products online, they will look for your corporate website. Your website content is what a potential reviewer or journalist, customers, investors or even employees see first and it is important to make a good first impression. Make sure that your website content includes information on products and product reviews as well as videos and podcasts. Also,

share positive posts by bloggers or reviewers on the website. Enable user-generated content and comments, add 'share this' buttons and enable RSS subscription.

Building a connection with your customers can have surprising results. Take the example of Threadless, a community-centered online apparel store based in Chicago, Illinois. One of its customers loves the brand enough to have built a <u>blog</u> which promotes and markets Threadless products.

<u>Select your social network carefully</u>
Be selective while choosing social networks for your company. Instead of popularity, relevance must be the basis for selection. There is no point in having a Facebook or MySpace account when your customers aren't visiting these sites. You would only be wasting your time and efforts and your brand would be severely out of touch.

Rather than choosing the more popular networks, look for the networks where your customers and employees hang out and interact. Create a company profile on social networks where there are lively discussions about your company or products. These are the networks which can help you build brand loyalty as well as influence your brand reputation. You could also build your own social network where your employees, customers and associates can socialize and discuss. Ning.com is a great site which helps companies to create their own social network.

<u>Choose your blog voice carefully</u>
A company blog is a great and accessible way to bolster and manage your company's online reputation. With your blog, you can interact and discuss with your customers and receive valuable feedback. It can be a team blog with your employees as the focus instead of your products or services. Existing and potential customers will relate better to the different tones and topics that your blog will present.
However, it is up to you to decide which style is more compatible to your business.

<u>Leave comments on blogs</u>
Which self-respectable blogger doesn't like comments? For bloggers, receiving a positive or perceptive comment is like an acknowledgement. Bloggers are more than happy to respond in kind by commenting back on your blog or subscribing and linking to your blog. It pays to invest some time to leave consistent comments on various blogs in your industry. This will help bloggers and their readers to get to know you and your brand. Computer hardware giant Dell learned it the painful way.

<u>Bloggers make good PR</u>
Check out blogs at <u>Technorati.com</u> or <u>Icerocket.com</u> and search for conversations

happening around your brand. Bloggers are people and sometime, they could be your customers. Bloggers are also very effective opinion-builders. Listen to them. Contact the influential bloggers, comment on their posts, and always be polite in your interactions. Establishing a personal connection with bloggers will help you during crunch times. They will be honest with you about any flaws in your product or service and will discuss it with you first instead of instantly publishing a negative post. And when they do publish a critical post, they will be less severe with you.

In a situation where your company is facing the ire of the blogosphere, do not deny the problem and take cover in the hope that the issue will die down on its own eventually. It will only get worse. As soon as you notice that your company's reputation is taking a beating, act immediately. Comment on the blog posts clarifying the issue and sign off with your email ID and a note that the poster can contact you for any further details. Write a blog post or record a video to discuss the problem as well as to announce any measures that you are taking to resolve the issue. Be sure to act fast. Any delay could not only result in a damaged reputation but it will also hurt your sales and popular opinion about your company.

Invite people to interact
Apple is one of the big companies to have openly expressed its disdain for Social Media, despite creating the iTunes and an active hand in popularizing podcasting. It bans its employees from blogging and sued some bloggers, who were amongst its biggest fans, for leaking data about products in development. The company even closed down online forums when people complained about problems with its operating system. By all accounts, the brand's image should have been hurt. But it wasn't. Why? The answer lies is in its customers who are also its ardent supporters. Apple has not felt the need to convince its users. When a brand is this strong, it does not have to try too hard to keep up with the rest.

But Apple is an aberration. Even big corporations like Nike, GM, Comcast and Dell have paid the price for neglecting Social Media. For entrepreneurs, the stakes are higher. You have to keep up a relentless communication with your industry and potential customers to survive the competition. For small companies, talking with your customers about your products or services beats any input from an expensive consultant. Never ignore your customers, either on your blog, Twitter or other social networks. And do not hesitate to ask for advice and suggestions from your customers.

Write, submit articles
Writing articles for magazines, online sources or blogs is a valuable public relations

tactic. You can work out a schedule so that your articles are submitted regularly. You can also submit your articles to online article directories like ezinearticles.com and articlesavenue.com. These sources can help increase your brand visibility in new places as well as promote your existing products.

Avoid spam
Sending spam is a great way to ruin your brand image. Mindless self-promotion will upset your fans and community members, even your friends. They will begin to associate you with spamming, will stop listening to you and altogether ignore you. And then you have to work twice as hard and spend twice as much to undo the damage.

Understand and rectify flaws
As a CEO or an entrepreneur, you have to recognize the flaws in your products or services. By understanding your weaknesses, you will be better prepared to respond faster in case of any attacks on that aspect of your business. In our internet age, quick responses can make or break your brand's reputation. Of course, do not be so hasty that your response is rude or off the topic.

It is never too late to create positive content that will show up on search results on sites like Ask.com, Bing and especially Google. Everyone turns to Google for information – clients, partners, investors, and even journalists. Hence, having your webpage or blog posts appear high on the first page of Google can help in reputation building.

**Monitor your online reputation, several times daily**
There is the incident of a laptop battery catching fire at the Los Angeles Airport. Immediately, there were internet reports suggesting that the laptop was a Thinkpad. Lenovo's reputation monitoring team acted quickly, identified the battery was not manufactured by them and spread that message. The company's quick response ensured there was no negative consumer sentiment against its Thinkpad series.

It pays to be slightly paranoid in this virtual age. The internet encourages people to communicate and offer opinions. A single disparaging remark or comment about your brand can cause damage if you do not find it and address it immediately. It is important to monitor your online reputation as often as possible, even several times a day. At anytime there could be people sharing complaints, exchanging customer service stories and asking questions about your products or services. There are several Internet sites and platforms where consumers can discuss their thoughts about companies. You can choose from the many online reputation monitoring tools available to monitor your company's reputation. For starters, even a Google Alert will do.

**Challenge: Use discretion in dealing with complaints**
In 2010, film director Kevin Smith tweeted that he was kicked off a Southwest Airlines flight for being "too fat." The story was picked up by several mainstream media outlets like the Wall Street Journal, USA Today and ABC News among others. Southwest took to their blog and Twitter account to issue apologies to Smith. They also issued several requests to send them direct messages if he required more help. Social Media can help companies to sort out bad customer experiences: Southwest's constant messages to Smith kept the issue alive across the web which resulted in everyone chiming in on the conversation. Companies have to work out how to tackle complaints from disgruntled customers with lots of visibility across the web.

**Brand monitoring tools**
Social Media, in many ways, complements traditional Public Relations, as it enables consumer engagement as well as dialogue between customers and companies. Let us examine some popular Social Media measures you must undertake to begin online reputation management of your brand.

Google Alerts
Google Alerts are email updates of the latest relevant Google results based on your choice of query or topic. The alerts monitor blog posts, articles, videos and discussion forums and groups. You can subscribe to them through email and RSS. Once you set a 'comprehensive alert,' it will report stories for your name, topic, and company. Google reader is also a good tool as it is easy to sort feeds, bookmark/favorite them and share them with your network.

Yahoo! Pipes is also a good tool for aggregating and combining feeds into one central repository.

Blogs
Create a business blog to help your company or organization interact with customers and share knowledge and expertise about the industry. Register your blog on Technorati or Delicious, which are amongst the world's largest blog search engines. You can track your brand on Technorati through search results of your brand. Subscribe to RSS alerts so that you are notified when someone blogs about you. Technorati also tracks blogs that link to yours. You can also monitor blog comments

using tools like Blacktype or coComment. Blacktype is an online application that allows you to follow and track the comments of your favorites or influential bloggers in your industry. With Blacktype, you can find, follow and share comments that people make on blog posts mentioning you or your brand. You can also subscribe to these comments using RSS.

## Twitter

Twitter is a fast evolving social messaging platform where messages (or tweets) travel incredibly fast. You can use <u>Twitter search</u> to search for your name, your company and related topics and then subscribe to it via RSS. <u>TweetBeep</u> is another additional tool that can send you email alerts. It is important to regularly monitor Twitter for reviews or complaints about your brand as it can influence opinions quickly and effectively. Based on the nature of the tweets, you can decide to either respond back or ignore it. Make sure that your tweets talk about the human side of your company. Have more than one person at your company handle tweets so that the account continues even if someone quits or takes a vacation.

Soulplantation, a San Diego-based restaurant chain, specializes in fresh soups and salads and has a very successful Twitter feed. The restaurants use Twitter to hold trivia contests and the first respondent wins coupons and free meals. They also post recipes and other information related to the restaurant. So far, the restaurant chain has over 14,000 followers and claims that Twitter has caused a 5-10% increase in foot traffic in the restaurant.

## Discussion Boards

Discussion boards are another channel where people can form a community to talk about you. Most sites pick up information from comments on these boards. You can use <u>boardtracker.com</u> to track threads mentioning your name. <u>Boardreader</u> is another tool that performs a similar role. You have to keep people's attention. Social Media not only helps you compete with your industry rivals but also with the internet where so much unique interactive content is posted every minute to grab people's attention.

## Social Comments

With <u>Yacktrack,</u> you can search for comments received on your content from sources like Blogger, Digg, StumbleUpon, or Wordpress blogs. For example, you have commented on a blog post but had to go offline for a while. Using Yacktrack, you can locate other commenters on the same post and rejoin the conversation. Yacktrack has a 'Chatter' tab with which you can perform keyword searches on Social Media sites for mentions of your brand name. You can also get an RSS feed for the search terms. <u>co.mments</u> is another similar tool.

## Social Media search engines

Social Mention:
This Social Media search engine that aggregates and tracks relevant results from Social Media sources like blogs, bookmarks, news, videos, and microblogging services. As with other tools, you can subscribe to your results by RSS or email. Serph and Keotag are other Social Media search engines.

Filtrbox
It delivers only the most relevant mentions of your key searches rather than thousands of random mentions of your brand. It tracks content based on contextual relevance, popularity and feedback.

Besides setting up alerts, you must focus on building relationships to monitor your brand. A dynamic network, especially if it includes people from your industry, will notify you of important updates without your request. For example, Pizza Hut has 1.2 million Facebook fans, while Domino's has 540,000. Domino's posts a few ads on their page which will get you momentary attention. Pizza Hut offers mobile apps, menus, coupons, and constant updates which not only gets it attention but brings in fans and regular visitors.

Listening to the online conversations about your brand should become a part of your daily research. Pay close attention to blog posts, tweets and discussion forums. Delegate an employee or yourself to manage and respond to online conversations about your brand or company. If you are a larger company, you can hire a professional to use the tracking tools.

Once you have selected your tracking tools, chalk out a schedule to check your RSS and email alerts, run searches for your name, company and relevant topics and respond to comments or posts. Being paranoid about your brand's image is a good thing. You have to be proactive to prevent negative reviews from spreading, to network with people of similar interests, to acknowledge praises, and to share positive feedback.

Reputation management is part of the communication process which can help your business grow. The status of your brand is always a key factor in winning new projects or in looking for new investors in your company. With every project, the image of your company and brand will shift and the importance of brand management and maintenance will increase.

**In conclusion:**
Reputation maintenance can help small businesses to understand consumers and their requirements by learning what they think about your products or services. The best way to directly engage with your customers is to create platforms for them where you can listen to your customers interacting and discussing your brand. Use the internet to check and read customer views about your product or service and recognize how and when opinions are being formed and influenced. Recognize that keywords can boost search results about your products or services and thus, help form perceptions about your company and accordingly, revamp your websites and blogs. It is also important that you are aware of your competitors and how customers perceive their products and services. You can use several available Internet tools to engage in effective PR for your brand.

**In the next chapter:**
You will be introduced to Social Media metrics that can help measure your online marketing success, and we will discuss why this is a vital part of your online marketing strategy. We will talk about the various web analytics software and other tools that measure Social Media traffic. The chapter will also look at setting benchmarks to measure Social Media marketing success.

## Chapter 14

# Measuring Social Media Marketing Success (Web Analytics, Google Analytics, etc.)

# Measuring Social Media Marketing Success

"What kind of metrics do you use to judge your success in the Web 2.0 world"? This is what Mike Moran asked Milind Mody, CEO of Ebrandz, as part of an interview published on Biznology Blog. We can tell you that this is probably one of the most important questions faced by all Social Media marketers. Because when it is an online medium, people always expect numbers to show a healthy Return on Investment (ROI). However, a good Social Media campaign is always a great 'branding' opportunity for a business, especially if it is a small business. Hence, the success or failure of a Social Media Marketing campaign cannot be based on pure numbers.

Mody's answer to the question was: "Social Media metrics is a moving target. But the success of the campaign should be judged not only on quantity but also on the quality of engagement. The quality part should be measured by asking these questions:
• Are we able to take part in conversations about our company and its products?
• Are we able to build better relationships with our audience?
• How are we perceived versus our competitors? "

So how do we define a successful Social Media marketing campaign? In this chapter, we will attempt to answer this question.

## The need for Social Media Metrics

Companies worldwide are adopting Social Media for online marketing campaigns and even involving employee participation. However, the question worrying them is how to measure ROI (Return on Investment) as well as what metrics to measure to base their campaigns' successes or failures. After all, you cannot measure the effectiveness of your Social Media campaigns if you are not measuring any metrics.

According to the 2009 Mzinga & Babson Executive Education study, over 80% of professionals do not measure ROI for their company's Social Media programs. This lag can be explained through understanding that social metrics and other measurement techniques are a relatively new field. Even so, there are organizations that are measuring social metrics, which eventually enables them to measure ROI. A Marketing Sherpa survey of over 2,000 marketers shows that the top three social metrics being monitored are:
1. Visitors and sources of traffic
2. Network size (followers, fans, members)
3. Quantity of commentary about brand or product

Social metrics will only be valuable to your business if you track, analyze and apply relevant metrics for a more effective Social Media marketing strategy. While each company will have some specific requirements, these are some common social metrics that can be applicable to each company. Let's discuss some important Social Metrics for companies:

**Monitor traffic from all Social Media sources**
Monitor and breakdown web traffic from all Social Media sources, and track the top sources over a period of time. Also track any referrals that the members of your Social Media networks are sending – this is very valuable data.

Bounce rate data can show you the way
Do you have any data about the visitors coming to your site from various Social Media sites but leaving quickly? The bounce rate data is vital as it can alert you to your site's shortcomings. Find the reasons for the short stay of visitors. Can a better landing page help tackle the issue? Explore the possibility. You can also address the issue by having more relevant copy and making it easy for visitors to navigate and find appropriate information.

Engagement duration data
For some companies, the duration of visitor engagement is more important than total page views. For example, if your company has a Facebook application, you can track the amount of time spent on it by members of your social network. Of course, you can deem your application a success if you see an increase in usage by members over a period of time. If your company's Social Media sites are directing visitors to your company websites, monitor the amount of time they are spending and the specific pages they visit.

Growth in Social Media membership
Monitor regularly to see if there is an increase in the active membership of your Social Media presence on networks like Facebook and Twitter. Check if there has been an increase in followers, fans and members as well as the level of active interaction with your Social Media content on these networks.

Interaction via blogs
Blogs can be a part of your Social Media marketing. For this, you have to allow comments and interact with readers by responding. This encourages responses either directly in the comments section of blog posts, or via Twitter by using blog widgets. Install blog plug-ins based on your blog's content. You can display the necessary sharing "buttons" like Digg or StumbleUpon on your blog posts. These

can help you track referrals back from these sites.

### Interaction level among members

The key is to measure how many members in your company's collective social network are actively interacting with others. Find the number of active members against total members and compare this ratio over a period of time. You cannot ensure that every single member is active at some point in time – some people will be inactive. However, you can get most people to begin interactions by initiating a campaign or contest or launching an application. Measure the resulting data for a change in the ratio. Keep interaction levels high or at least consistent among members to keep their interest alive.

### Conversions

Ideally, your social network membership should convert into subscriptions, sales - direct or through affiliates, increased usage of Facebook applications among other sales offerings that can be directly or indirectly monetized. For example, subscription to e-newsletters can be monetized by giving other companies access to your list in the form of advertising. You can measure all kinds of conversions and compare them over a period of time.

### Brand chatter in social media

A highly active social network and membership means increased chatter about your company or your brands. You can measure and track both positive and negative mentions, and their quantities.

### Sharing

Social networks can also help members and fans to interact in the network repeatedly by sharing content and links, talking about your brands and promoting your brands or products. You can measure how many members re-share content and how often they do so.

### Monitor virals

Viral marketing and word-of-mouth publicity is the key in Social Media networks. Your social members will be sharing Twitter tweets and Facebook updates relevant to your company. You have to monitor this if information is being re-shared by their networks. Find out the time lapse before re-sharing and then how many friends of friends are re-sharing your links and content. This will help you figure out what kind of content has a better chance of going viral and initiating conversations.

The above list is indicative and depending on your business objectives, you can use all or any combination of these key metrics to monitor and analyze. These are not easy or simple to track and you will need custom tools and reports to gather and analyze the data. Resulting data from every Social Media initiative or campaign must be measured based on specific goals. These can be the amount of application usage and the resulting conversions. You can use Multiple Moving Averages (MMAs) to show both short and long-term trends, which can provide you an overall view of the success of your sites and social networks.

**Define your goals**

It is crucial to define your company's bottom line in regards to its Social Media strategy before taking the plunge. For example, the goal should not be to have a huge number of Facebook fans or Twitter followers. The key is to be able to smartly track members and keep them active over a longer period of time. For example, if you are keen to use Twitter to increase traffic to your blogs or sites, your goals must include link sharing, retweets, hashtag campaigns, referrals, contests and giveaways, followers, and tweets measured per day, week and month. Equally important is to set down specific goals for your team. The goals must be realistic and achievable, like the number of expected new followers each month with well-thought tactics to increase membership over a sustained period of time.

**Select tracking tools**
You can use a combination of several tools to create a system which works for your small business. These tools can generate insightful graphs which can track specific campaigns. Let's look at some of these tools:

Hootsuite
A web-based Twitter client designed for professional users. You can use this application to view user information, automatically feed your blog through Twitter, save Twitter searches and groups as columns, embed your columns as and where required and schedule tweets. By integrating with the HootSuite URL shortener, you can get graphs and demographics for users who click on your shared links. You also get graphs for clicks, top referrers and other information on individual tweets.

Tweetmeme
Use Tweetmeme retweet buttons to encourage visitors to retweet your blog posts as well as track shares via retweets and bit.ly analytics.

Bit.ly
This is Twitter's popular URL shortener. It can give an insight into the performance of

your shared links. Bit.ly can provide click data, location details, referrer information and other related conversations.

### Trendrr
This is a great tracking tool for small businesses. Their data sources include blogs, microblogs, search, social networks and even videos. Trendrr can be used to track Twitter search results, as well as user stats for following, followers, and updates daily. Their Twitter post report helps view tweet count fluctuation daily during a campaign.

**Prepare reports**
Once you have finalized your strategies and selected suitable tracking tools, you can set up ongoing reports. Set up custom reports, which can measure against your goals, and update them regularly. The more experience you garner about using these applications, the more you will increasingly refine your objectives and reports.

**Tools to measure Social Media traffic**
Web analytics enable gathering and analyzing your web content data to collect meaningful information about how your company's websites are being utilized by members, fans and other users. A key point to remember is that Social Media isn't always about numbers, graphs and charts. It is more to do with perception, engagement and emotions. Monitoring Social Media at this point is like dealing with volatile signals. There are many different Web analytics applications available. While these attempt to pin down numbers, brand perceptions and engagement ratios, we need more intelligent applications to figure out the intangible details.

**Google Analytics** is the most powerful free software in this area. This application can measure the traffic generated to your website and demographics details. With Google Analytics, you can the view number of visitors to your site during a specified time frame. You can find out if whether they found your sites through a search engine or they were referred by another website. You can also see details like how long visitors stayed on your website, the pages they visited, links clicked, number of visitors who bounced away from a page or stayed there longer. Bounce rates can tell you which pages require better content to make them more visitor-friendly.

It has an easy-to-use interface, and even offers e-commerce statistics which are usually not available in free applications. You can also use this application to compare the data from other tools like Twitter Counter with your website's traffic stats to find out if a tweet that generated higher levels of followers also increased traffic to your website. Google Analytics has another powerful feature called Advanced Segments which can allow you to group certain kinds of visits together in your data. This is useful while measuring traffic and conversions from social media. For example, you can create a custom segment for Twitter, Digg and Facebook. This will help you determine amount and quality of traffic and conversions from social media.

Google Analytics undergoes constant updates and is a critical resource in your search marketing campaign. It can show you valuable data about your visitors that you can use in combination with your Google Sitemap and other Google services. With Google Analytics, you can use this data together with AdWords and AdSense data to optimize your campaigns.

Some free solutions software includes AWStats, Facebook Insights and Twitter Counter. These do not offer you much support compared to paid software, but these are good options if you want to gain some experience before selecting paid software. Let's take a look at some of these.

**Facebook insights** allows Facebook Page administrators to measure the number of likes, dislikes, active users and interactions their page receives over a period of time. It offers demographic details of your fans like gender, age, location and language; the page activity including video plays, audio plays, and photo views. This application can help you evaluate which posts, photos or videos raised the most interest among your fans leading to a better understanding of your market.

**Twitter Counter** helps track your Twitter history over a period of a week, month or a quarter (3 months). This can help you figure out which of your tweets had the biggest impact on your following. Twitter Counter also helps compare your stats with your competitors and enables you to measure your efforts against theirs.

**YouTube Insight:** You can track various statistics of your uploaded video content using YouTube Insight http://www.youtube.com/. This application can offer a range of information like demographics of your audience, community stats, amount of views over a year, how people found your video and the variances in viewership at each moment in your video. This can be a useful tool if you want to use YouTube to launch viral campaigns to measure their viewability or understand the popularity of different videos, based on time and location. With this, you can find out what your audience likes and you can build campaigns based on it.

**WordPress blog stats:** The popular WordPress blog stats http://wordpress.org/extend/plugins/stats/ can help bloggers understand what content their audiences enjoy the most or least about your blog. Wordpress blog stats give you an insight on numbers of views, top referring links, most viewed pages and posts, top search engine terms and number of shares among Social Media networks. You can also see what subscribers to your blog are clicking on and viewing from your blog.

**Omniture's SiteCatalyst** is a popular paid software, a market leader in the field of advanced web analytics. You can customize Omniture to collect and analyze and map out the data of your website traffic. The reports can help you measure your online objectives and marketing activities. With Omniture, you can visualize the traffic on your website, specific success factors can be defined and applications can be measured. You can also generate reports about defined visitor segments. Its dashboard segment helps you get immediate insights into the most important reports.

If your company has a presence in more than one Social Media channels, you can utilize these tools to understand your market and figure out what works for your audiences in each channel so as to improve the success of your content.

### Benchmarks to measure Social Media Marketing success

The success of your Social Media marketing depends on the aims of each of your campaigns. We discuss below some of the common measurements that apply equally to Social Media as well as other marketing channels. All of these may not be appropriate for each campaign but you can consider a combination of these while considering measurement.

Rise in revenue
This is a very straightforward measure. Checking your rise in revenue helps you measure the amount of business done before the Social Media campaign and the level of business after the campaign launch. Looking at revenue can provide one way to see whether the campaign helped to increase business or whether business fell or remained constant.

Advantage against competitors
You can check which competitors of yours are running Social Media campaigns. Conduct a before-and-after comparison against your competitors. Are they doing better on the Social Media channels compared to you? Have their Social Media campaigns brought in more tangible results versus your campaign results? Comparing data will help you understand who has the competitive advantage and how you stack up.

Increase in number of visitors
Another measure of the success of your Social Media campaign is the total number

of visitors to your company websites. Check and compare if the number of visitors have increased since launching the campaign. You can also find out more details about them like their demographics by breaking the visitors down by channel using referral data. This will allow you to know if your visitors are the right demographic for your brand and company.

Word-of-mouth
This is the most difficult metric to measure. Research companies like Neilsen use Buzz Metrics and Blog Pulse to measure the number of people talking about a brand or company. You can also use Google Trends to identify attention spikes across the web. Using these, you can find out if mentions of your brand have increased after a campaign as well as on which Social Media channels these mentions occur.

Search
You can measure if more people have searched for your brand or company or product after a particular Social Media campaign. The keywords searched by people can help you measure which message or products have received more queries. This will allow you to understand the requirements of your target audience.

Links
Similarly, links are another good measure of the success of a Social Media campaign. After a campaign launch, find out if your websites or blog posts or fan pages have received more links. Combined with SEO, links provide a fillip to your Social Media presence. Social Media is a powerful link building method. Links assure that your messages are carried across the net.

Market research
This is mostly conducted by larger companies as they have the resources to conduct a huge study. They can contact a research group to conduct field studies, focus groups, and interviews to find out the level of brand awareness among target groups.

**In conclusion:**
Companies must realize that understanding Social Media metrics is an excellent way to understand the importance of social media. There are a lot of businesses, especially small business, who are yet to get involved in social media. Perhaps, because the huge amount of noise surrounding Social Media these days intimidates them. Getting involved in Social Media is about building up marketing campaigns based on carefully devised metrics. This chapter will hopefully encourage business owners to embrace social media.

Measuring Social Media has become an important feature for companies engaged in Social Media campaigns. More than the connection with their audience, companies are rather keen to measure the return on investment (ROI). But the very nature of Social Media makes it difficult to reliably calculate metrics. It is better to ask if you are causing a conversation and if your sales have seen an increase. These are what ultimately a company looks for from a campaign. The other aspects only aid in achieving your bottom line.

**In the next chapter:**
We will discuss website conversions and why your website needs conversion optimization. We will also look into the importance of testing, analysis and user personas, and we will examine various steps and strategies to optimize your website to achieve better business results.

## Chapter 15

# How to Increase Website Conversions

# How to Increase Website Conversions

"Was just talking about usability vs. conversion optimization and the fact that the latter always wins in any conflict of ideas..." goes an eBrandz tweet. As writers of this book, we debated about having a chapter on 'Website Conversions' in a book which talks primarily about Social Media Marketing for small business. But we concluded that Website Conversion Optimization was too important a topic to be ignored. As a business owner, if you are aware of conversion optimization, you can make a better informed decision on whether to spend your money on getting more traffic or increasing your website conversions. In many cases, converting more traffic is a better option than spending money to get more traffic.

Medalia Art, a New York-based art gallery, sells Brazilian and Caribbean art online. As an online seller, they showcase paintings from three famous artists on their homepage. The company decided to test what would happen if they replaced the paintings with photos of the artists themselves. The goal, here, was to increase visitor engagement and reduce bounce rates. With the photos of paintings, the company noticed a conversion rate of 8.8% but when replaced with artists' photos, the conversion rate rose by almost 90% with an increase of 17.2%.

You need to go through your website and make sure to include principles of Website Conversion and then start conversion optimization.

### So what exactly is Website Conversion?
Most company websites are often built with the sole aim to increase their traffic. The question is -- your website might be generating a healthy traffic, but is it generating business? Website conversation rate measures the percentage of webpage visitors who turn into customers. It measures the number of people who purchase your products and services through your website.

Conversion rate optimization is a process which will help your website to lower the bounce rate percentage and convinces a visitor to take an action that you want them to take every time. When we say "conversion rate," we mean the percentage of visitors that arrive at a page and convert into potential customers or leads, instead of abandoning the site. This concept is different than that of search engine optimization, which focuses on getting the best possible search engine ranking for the same page.

When it comes to conversions, you're trying to impress humans, instead of crawlers. The two goals of decreasing the bounce rate and increasing potential customers can be achieved successfully as long as your SEO specialist is trained in the art of both and the search terms you're optimizing to drive the type of people who are likely to convert. We shall first discuss some of the most common flaws found on the websites that hinder conversion Optimization:

**Bad Website structure:** The structure of the website is not well organized or the message is not kept consistent across all important pages. Due to this many visitors abandon the site from the homepage itself.

**Buying cycle not optimized:** Sometimes the buying process is either too long or is difficult to start with.

**Missing contact details or unduly long contact form:** The most common thing that helps the visitors get in touch with you is your contact number or the lead form. It's often either missing or hidden within the inner pages. There are a lot of unnecessary fields in the form. Many site visitors seek minute details, which leads to low conversion rates.

**Copy not properly optimized:** Copies on many websites are not well optimized. Either they talk about themselves or there is a thesis of content on the service or product. Some of them don't have headlines or have one that doesn't motivate the visitor to hold on to the page. This leads to high bounce rates.

**Credible elements missing from the site:** Many websites fail to highlight their testimonials, certifications, media comments or security logos. These are some of the most important factors that motivate the visitor to make purchases from your website.

**Website Optimizer**
After investing in driving traffic to your website, you must now set up mechanisms to track conversions and calculate conversion rates. Without effective tracking software, you cannot measure what aspects to improve. There are two popular services – Google Website Optimizer and Visual Website Optimizer.

One important piece of data that can help you restructure your website is the bounce rate – the number visitors who leave the site without much activity. A lower bounce rate means that visitors are using the site effectively. You can also use tools like Google Analytics to track how effectively your content is in converting visitors to customers. However, tracking will not help you figure out the best content for your site – that can only be done by testing different content.

Website Optimizer can help you study the effects of different content on your users. Testing will allow you to identify the content that elicits the best response from users and to ensure that your website is more effective in getting the desired business results. Website Optimizer software can help you improve the effectiveness of your website and the return on your investment by testing if changes to your website's content are more effective in getting conversions. You can choose a web page or parts of a page -- headline, image and promotional text – for testing which content on your site users respond to best.

Website Optimizer can help improve your conversion rate and increase your return on investment by enabling you to figure out what users on your site respond to best. With this software, you can show your website's visitors multiple versions of a page or elements on a page to test which pages or elements are most effective.

**Steps and strategies**
A user-friendly website can have a huge effect on converting visitors to sales, thus improving the site's bottom line and delivering a higher ROI. The focus should be to make the conversion process quick and easy. More conversions will help your business make more profits. Let's take a look at some measures that you can take to sell better online and convert more visitors to potential sales.

**Understanding your target visitors**
Understanding your target visitors is an important factor in the success of a particular webpage. While developers and designers might talk about it, much less attention is given to implementing it. Begin with understanding your target market and then use the marketing data to create site user personas. You have to understand the motivations, desires and concerns of your customers regarding your products or services. Then, you can build a webpage that focuses on converting these visitors to customers. If you do not research your audience properly, then the greatest design will not be able to save your campaign.

User Personas
The technique of User Personas is used to simulate the behaviours of users to interact with web pages and to reach their goals. A user persona is a fictitious representation of your targeted website visitors. Personas allow you to figure out problems with different website elements like design, navigation, content, forms and the conversion process. Personas help to put a human face on a group of visitors with certain desires and behaviors, seeking certain goals. This can help you design your webpage layouts, navigation and call-to-actions, to meet their requirements.

Why do you need user personas?
You can optimize your website based on simple demographics, but it will not allow you to understand your users enough to identify their motivations, preferences and online behavior. For example, let's say that your target clients are 25-35 years old, white, college-educated women. How can this demographical information affect the design and elements on your website main page? And if you are targeting men who are 30 years old, white, and enjoy shopping and searches by brands – your website elements will need to be different for this different demographic. Personalizing a user makes you relate to them and optimize your site accordingly. The more information you gather, the better equipped you will be at catering the site to their needs.

Personas are usually developed on the basis of information collected from Google Analytics, interviews with actual clients and demographics from your market research. A definition of each persona should include statistics like background, attitudes, goals, levels of internet experience and others. The personas need to seem as real as possible. Persona background should include name, photo, age, gender, education and work experience as well as personality, communication style and computer skills. Each persona should cite the expectations and goals for coming to the website and what problems they face while looking for what they need on the site. Importantly, personas must include user's urgency of requirements/desires and whether they are motivated most by price or quality.

Designing your website based on customer experience increases trust and leads to better conversion rates. This is how it can be achieved.

**Improve the clarity of your website**
Identify the main objective of your website and present it in a way that prompts visitors to dig in for more information. For instance, include headlines, offers and discounts. It's better to have a headline such as "8 reasons why you should select eBrandz over other SEO companies" rather than a plain "Search Engine Optimization Service." If your visitor doesn't like the headline, they won't read any further. A simple-yet-effective approach is to express your main message in a headline. Fill the copy with tangible benefits and not only fancy features.

**Landing page**
A page at which your visitors arrive through a text or banner ad or through the organic search is called a landing page. In simple words it's likely your first and last opportunity to start a conversation with your visitors. There is a misconception that a landing page is a standalone page, without any navigation or that it's detached from the website. Sometimes a single page is sufficient to achieve the goal and other

times you may have to create a series of pages, each with a conversion event that leads to the ultimate goal.

### Images on landing page
Choose graphics that will enhance the design of your landing page. It is suggested that you use graphics and colors similar to those used in any promotional creative relating to your product or service. Changing the colors or graphics with which your customer has become acquainted can cause confusion and the customer could click away from the site.

### Don't go overboard with design
You do not have to use the latest web graphics merely because they are the latest. Often, simple and clean designs help to focus visitors to complete the desired action on the page. Too many graphics could distract them and cause your message to be lost. Also, a heavy landing page will take longer time to load and your visitors may not be patient enough to wait.

### Powerful headline on landing page
When a visitor first arrives on your site, apart from the design and brand name, it is the headline of the page that influences decisions to engage with your page. A powerful headline can draw visitor attention, compel them into reading the page and checking further webpages. Create several headlines and test them against each other to see which one works best with your users.

CityCliq, a Florida-based startup, conducted a split test on how best to position their product on the homepage. They tested a variety of headlines, like:
• Businesses grow faster online!
• Get found faster!
• Online advertising that works!
• Create a webpage for your business

Which do you think worked? The headline "Create a webpage for your business" arouses interest and the visitor will stay to look at the other content on the page. And that is what it did. This headline helped CityCliq increase conversions by 90%. Why? Because the headline is clear and to the point and said what CityCliq does exactly while the others were too generic and failed to clarify the goals of the company. A similar example of a convincing headline is "30-day Free Trial on All Accounts" while "Start a High-Rise Account" does not have the same clear message.

## Simplify site navigation

Complicated navigation causes user frustration and lower conversion rates. Help visitors to quickly and easily find the products and services that they are searching for by categorizing your items into brand, price or other relevant groupings. Making customers navigate between several pages in order to make a purchase increases the likelihood of abandonment of the shopping cart. Improve the flow of buying process; this will help you increase the number of sales.

## Check Call-to-Action

Your call-to-action copy, i.e. copy that tells the user what to do, should be compelling to convert visitors. These can be at the end of your sales copy. Make the offer and tell the visitor what they want to do and why they want to. While writing your call-to-action, remember that you are optimizing for a busy visitor. If they cannot locate how to try out your offering, they will hit the back button. And you don't want that! These should be clear and concise like "begin now" or "get started today" rather than just "submit." Toronto start-up Dmix tested "Signup for free" and "Get Started Now" for their sign up button and found the latter had more conversions.

Another way is to have your call-to-action copy on colored buttons, preferably bright colors like red because they are eye catching and drive attention toward them. Dmix also tested the "Get Started Now" copy against green and red buttons and found out that the red colored button worked more effectively. Remember, changing your call-to-action buttons doesn't necessarily guarantee the highest return on investment from your website, but it surely communicates what you want your visitors to do when they arrive at that page.

## Make information easy to find, consistent

Make sure that your visitors find the information they expect. Your promotional messages should always lead to relevant pages and not to the homepage. You only have seconds to hold a customer's focus and you cannot risk it by forcing a visitor to search for information. Your promo landing page should have similar graphics to the promotional message. If your promo message on your homepage says "10% off on all photo prints," then the promo landing page should have the same message. Otherwise, you run the risk of confusing the user and forcing him to back click from your page.

Medalia Art also conducted an earlier test to optimize the bounce rate to their homepage by changing the placement of their Holiday Sale promotional message. Discounts often encourage more visitors to go through multiple webpages to explore different products. In order to determine the best location on the homepage for the message, they conducted a split test – where different visitors see different versions of the homepage. One version had "Holiday Sale" displayed in big, red font on the top of the homepage. The second version had the message in a sidebar with small font.

They split the testing tools to track conversion rate rather than the bounce rate. So to track bounce rate, Medalia Art defined a click on any link on the homepage as a conversion. For example, if the conversion rate was 45%, they calculated the bounce rate as 100-45 = 55%. When bounce rates were tracked, it was found that the prominent message had about 21% less bounce rate than the sidebar message. The lower bounce rate means more visitor interest in the paintings and potentially more sales. While initially there was a fear that the in-your-face promo might irritate visitors, it turned out to be the better version.

**Pay attention to product pages**
You have to invest time and effort to ensure optimization of your product pages. Test with showing the product in use or against a solid background. The 'product in use' style works for apparel companies or boutiques – it may not work as well if you are selling electronics. Placement of images on the page is also vital. Test with placing product images on the left and right sides of product pages and check which converts better. A zoom feature, allowing visitors to examine the product closely, can be a great addition.

- Each product must have 3-4 images but make sure that these are high quality images. If not photographed properly, it will turn off the visitor. The idea is to make the user want to possess the product. A single high quality image is better than multiple low quality ones.
- Product descriptions are important. Test different versions of copy, keeping in mind your market segment. For example, test the impact of non-technical copy against technical copy on users.
- Pricing is another important factor. Most online shoppers indulge in comparison shopping. You can test different prices and see their impact on your conversion rates.
- Tell visitors when they can have the product in their hands. For example, "Within 7 working days" sounds better to a potential customer than "between 3-10 days." Many e-commerce sites who offer free shipping on orders above a certain size usually see a good increase in conversions.

**Testimonials**
Nothing beats a concise, to the point and credible testimonial! Testimonials from

past customers can make prospective customers feel more at ease about doing business with you. Testimonials should be about the benefits of your services and relevant to your target audience. A credible testimonial should include full name, location, and perhaps, even a photo of the customer. Video testimonials are even more successful in converting visitors to customers. In general, a video testimonial is better than one with an image. Likewise, a testimonial with just an image is better than a testimonial with just a name, which in turn is better than an anonymous testimonial. This is one of the simplest ways of marketing your products or services for free. It will also help to increase the credibility of your website.

**Privacy**
If you are asking visitors for their email addresses, then promise them that their privacy will be guarded. If you are a B2C site and want clients to close the sale on the site, then make sure that your credit card processing pages are secure and hacker free. Your privacy policy should be clear and easy to understand. It should let them know that you are making the effort to safeguard their information. Direct your customers to your privacy policy. Near call-to-action, place a simple text saying "Your privacy is important to us" on the link to your privacy policy. It will help tremendously in converting them.

**Check your conversion funnels**
Every step that a visitor takes on your website to become a conversion is part of the conversion funnel. Check your conversion funnel and ensure that the entire process is simple, compelling and easy to complete.

**Keep online forms simple**
The conversion process must be as easy and simple as possible. Test various scenarios. For example, allow visitors to make purchases as guests, instead of registering with you. If there are online forms, limit the number of fields on them. If you only want to generate leads, request only their e-mail address and/or phone number. Ask only for information that is absolutely essential for your purposes. Or have the input cursor jump to the next field in the form on its own.

**Tools to analyze websites & their visitors behavior**

**Google Website Optimizer:** It is a free tool from Google which helps to test from a single element to an entire page of the website.

**Google Analytics:** It gives you an in-depth analysis of the entire website. It analyzes the current cost-per-conversion bounce rate of every page. It also studies the buying funnel, optimizing it to reduce the abandon rate and increase the conversion.

**Click Heat, Scroll reach and Mouse move map:** This tool will help to analyze where the users are actually clicking, and how many of them actually scroll down your page.

**User Testing:** It is done for usability testing. Here real visitors are tested on your website. Include a video of visitors voicing their thoughts as they use your site and a written summary of their problems encountered while navigating within your website. Let's learn more about it in the following paragraphs.

### Importance of usability testing

Testing is a very important aspect of the whole process. It allows you to analyze more than one website element at a time in order to determine which combinations lead to high conversions. Test different combinations of content, images, headlines and pricing in order to identify which elements consistently result in high conversion rates.

Usability testing is important if you need to prioritize the elements or pages that must be optimized first. Before starting usability testing, you have to identify a persona. Take, for example, the persona of John Mathison, 38, a long haul trucker who has an aggressive yet logical personality, not very web savvy, and takes his time while shopping. With this persona you can locate users that match this profile. The more specific personas you create, the easier it will be to locate actual users belonging to that category for usability testing. Say, you create 3 personas for a given website and select 5 individuals for each persona, this will help your usability test acquire a lot more insights about prioritizing elements to be optimized and how it should be optimized.

Online shopping can be an impersonal experience for users. But if you consider your users as individuals and can put a face, life and personality to your different demographic segments, optimizing for them will not seem like a daunting task. No longer will it just be a transaction; you will have just sold to Tonya Ramsey, 27, African-American, nurse who likes shopping but worries about costs.

Here are some of the common mistakes which should be avoided while testing.
- **Launching a re-design of your website:** Many web marketers assume that due to a bad web design, their website conversions will be poor so they think of redesigning the site. Launching a re-design of your website without measuring the

effect it has on your conversions may actually reduce the conversions. Instead analyze your visitor's behavior, and find out why the page is not able to engage them for a minimum time.

- **Testing the wrong elements and wrong pages on the website** – Never assume that by just changing the color of the button your conversion will be improved. There are few important reasons for doing so. Some of them complain that they never come across any improvement in conversion by testing different elements on the page. This is because they concentrate on changing the design layout or the color theme, and ignore crucial aspects like copy, headlines and lead form. First, identify the elements that require testing and optimize them to get positive results.

- It is important to see whether they support the unique value proposition. Your copy must be customer oriented. Many Internet marketing companies suggest that you test webpages to improve the conversion. But do you know which ones to test? Testing a wrong page will lead to wrong conclusions & also affect your overall conversion rate.

- **Overshooting the budget:** Resorting to expensive testing software even before they understand how to design high-converting web pages is a mistake that most website owners commonly make. Testing your webpages without following their objective will never improve their functionality and will only lead to inflated budgets.

## Practical examples to establish significance of successful conversion optimization

A debt consulting company, as part of its campaign, optimized the ad but not the landing page. The campaign failed to click. Analysis established that the headline was not appealing enough. It was quite confusing too. Also, the overall presentation including fonts was poor. The information was not properly organized; it didn't tell the visitors how the site could help them solve their problem. The form was a little bit congested, hence it did not attract visitors. The conversion rate was in the single digits. Once the optimized version was launched, the conversion rate went up more than four times.

In another case, just creating an appealing headline and presenting the features properly helped to increase the conversion rate. The call-to-action button too made a lot of difference. Inserting words "It's free" instead of "Join Now" made the visitors realize the benefit they had.

**In conclusion:**

Conversion optimization is important because traffic must convert into sales to affect your bottom line or else, it is just traffic. Conversion optimization is not about how much money you can invest; it requires equal dollops of creativity to make it work. As a small business, you may find yourself beaten at generating traffic by bigger competitors; however, you have an equal chance to beat them in the conversion rate game.

Each website has its own unique goals; so the approach to conversion rate optimization will be unique for all. What worked for one website may not work for another. So the main challenge`

# Chapter 16

# Conclusion

# Conclusion

In the zeal to maximize revenue and attract new customers to a small business by using and leveraging Social Media Marketing, we should not forget that the American dream has not divorced ethics from its ambit yet. It doesn't suffice to be just legally safe. Entrepreneurs and small-business owners should also play the game by ethically sound rules and operate with a clean conscience. This is a potent and long-lasting formula for building a small business successfully. There is definitely something in the saying "Honesty is the best policy" in social media marketing.

A challenge for any new Internet marketer is figuring out how to position him/herself in an industry climate which rewards experience and reputation. Be honest and tell your prospective customers that you are new to the industry, but emphasize the strength and experience of your team as well as your passion to achieve your goals. People respond to honesty and passion and when they realize that you are working to meet their best interests, they will be more open to your sales campaign.

Some new businesses think they can get away with initially faking their experiences or product reviews. It is important to remember that by joining a social network or getting yourself an online presence means you are joining a community. In a community, there is neither scope nor space for dishonesty, dissemination of false information, pushy advertising or invasion of privacy via spamming.

Very often, businesses in search of a quick buck forget about customer service. They will try to deceive the system while telling themselves that they are being honest. Social media companies have to tread the very thin line between integrity and deceit. Building an honest Internet marketing campaign always requires time and effort, but it will ensure customer retention and brand loyalty.

## Maintaining integrity in business

Integrity means keeping your word - doing what you have committed to do. Building a culture of integrity will inform your customers that for you, their satisfaction comes first and your profit bottom line second. This garners your customers' trust. If you are offering more value to your customers and offering a sincere customer service experience, you are building a campaign of integrity.

Always be honest and do not communicate false information. Today, social media marketing firms build their reputations on a commitment to integrity and customer service. As an Internet marketer, you must be careful not to mislead your potential clients or to lure clicks from members. Do not manipulate your advertising to impact income. Offer content of interest and genuine value to effectively promote your product. Anything less can really put a dent in your social media advertising campaign. Be frank about your newness in the industry.

You may lack experience but honesty, integrity and quality products and services can go a long way in creating a strong and winning online reputation for you. Delivering on your promises is important even if sometimes, it means loss of revenue in the short run. Timely delivery and business honesty will always benefit your business and give you a good reputation, which is more important in the long run than revenue.

To be a successful social media marketer, you have to be disciplined enough to handle every situation with integrity. Providing an unprejudiced view of your business and products – and this means not misleading potential customers – will help build a sustainable long term business.

## Some Pointers
You must keep certain points in mind while dealing with social media networks and communities:
- Every network and community has its own guidelines – understand them well and ensure that these are respected at all times.
- Do not use automated systems to distribute messages – social community members have less patience for any kind of non-personal communication or spamming.
- Always make full disclosure of affiliations, relationships and incentives in all social media networks. Withholding such information equals deceit in social media communities. Recognize that honesty is non-negotiable.
- If you are sending products for review to bloggers and other social media influencers, do not make the mistake of asking them to lie for any incentive. Trying to manipulate them is a surefire way to lose credibility.
- Be aware that merely sending them the products does not obligate them to review these and offer you coverage. You can send them products and encourage them to spread the word but the final decision lies with the influencers.
- Be prepared for honest product appraisals. You cannot influence what they tell the others about your products.
- Similarly, demand that the bloggers reveal the source of products under review. If disclosure doesn't happen, take immediate action and either educate the online influential about disclosures or withdraw your relationship with them.

These steps will ensure credibility of word-of-mouth promotion in social media marketing. A failure to recognize these steps will destroy reputations and relationships.

## Principle of "Six degrees of separation"
The 'six degrees of separation' (also known as the human web) states that, "a person is a step away from people they know and two steps distant from people known by the people they know and is therefore only six degrees away from anyone

in the world. You may have heard or even played the game "Six Degrees of Kevin Bacon" – the game was invented as a play on this concept. The American social psychologist Stanley Milgram measuring connectivity across the United States said he "discovered that only a small number of connections, especially through hubs and portals like the world wide web, interlink the entire population." Today, we are ever more connected than any other time. Networking is part of our lives now – the more people we get to know, the more publicity and promotion our works receive. And networking is the key to building long-term customers who can help develop a successful online small business.

Loyal customers bring more value to your business than just money. They act as evangelists and influencers who can introduce your products to new potential customers. By creating a dedicated customer base, you can become a profitable and influential brand. As a small business owner, you can utilize the six degrees of separation to gain customers for life. As per the theory, your company is just six degrees away from turning a non-customer into a customer for life.

**First impressions are important**
In today's extremely competitive climate, companies only have the one opportunity to make a good first impression. For an online small business, this first impression is formed when potential customers visit your website. Your website must be able to tell a visitor about your offerings at a glance. If they are unable to understand your exact services or are preoccupied by unnecessary site elements, they will either melt into the Internet or will be so distracted as to not make any purchases. Take a look at your company website now. What impression does it give you? Is it consistent with the message you want to send to a first time visitor? If you answered yes, your website is fine. If not, take a second look at it to make the message stand out.

**A simple purchase process**
Now that you have the attention of your potential customer, you have to get the visitor to make the actual purchase. Look at your website again. Does your website make it easy for a potential customer to view products as well as make the purchase? Is the purchase form simple or does it have several redundant sections? How long does it take the visitor to make a purchase? Online purchases should be a quick and simple process. A more complicated purchase process will turn your customers off your website.

**Clear call-for-action**
Your website content should promote your products and services with the aim to make an actual sale. Copy should appeal to your potential customers – avoid a cold

and bland approach. Try to use a conversational tone to arouse emotion in your visitors. Remember, talk to your customers, not at them.

**Spread the word**
You have to get people to talk about your business. This begins with you. Tell your friends about your new business; advertise it to them with passion and energy and the energy will rub off and they will be keen to share your message with their friends. Don't think to yourself: I will just let my work do the talking! For one thing, that means fewer people get to know about your business. Secondly, on the Internet and social media networks, it is your enthusiasm and belief in reaching your goals and helping others that will arouse emotions among prospective customers.

**Share your expertise and stay connected**
Another way for a small business owner to gain visibility and credibility online is to share your expertise with others on message boards and discussion forums. Offering advice and solutions on social sites will increase your following via word-of-mouth as well as project you as a credible source in your niche industry. This will help you develop a good relationship with your online customers and followers, which in turn will help your business to grow. Social media marketing helps businesses to share information, connect with existing customers and attract potential customers. Always keep your customers informed about any changes you make in your products, services or operations. Offer them a platform to ask queries and receive answers or advice on how to use your products or make the best use of your services. Your online business will continue to grow as your online relationships develop.

**Search Engine Optimization**
Keywords-driven traffic from search engines to your website is the best kind of traffic. Search engines like Google use algorithms to rank pages based on keywords, quality of content and the amount of backlinks received. If your website has been optimized for search engines, search engines will match your website with the keywords entered. Your website's rank on the search pages will depend on its backlinks, i.e. the number of times social media site users have bookmarked your site. This is a very good reason to have quality content on your website and to use well-researched keywords. One of the ways social media marketing can help your business is through social bookmarking – which is, submitting a link from your website on social media sites – a quick and easy process. However, the jury is still out on whether people on social media sites actually follow the links. Therefore, it is crucial that you select social media sites for your marketing campaigns after thoroughly researching existing communities for your niche. If there is a need for your services, you can target the niche communities and benefit from direct traffic.

**Bonus tip: Promote your personality to promote your business**
Social business networking is about promoting your personality. So be careful about not sounding boastful or rude. Your advertising and promotional campaigns should draw on your passion and enthusiasm for your business and your keen desire to make a difference in your niche. Any social media activities that you undertake must be in keeping with your brand values. Always put people first and focus on offering sterling customer service and satisfying their requirements. Research and design your service around their requirements. And of course, while selecting a catchy brand slogan for your business, ensure that the slogan speaks about you, your strengths and what makes you stand apart from the rest.

**Internet marketing – Do it right or don't do it at all!**
You have to recognize that the Internet can be a dangerous neighborhood; so you either do things right or don't do them at all. As an online business, you have to follow the rules of the internet – which can be quite different from conventional marketing. Always be firm but courteous while dealing with potential customers and community members. You have to be active on all social media sites where your business has a presence – as well as tough as nails to survive initial hiccups and failures. Learn from the mistakes – but be sure to learn fast! Correct any online mistakes at the earliest to minimize negative impact. Conduct continuous research into the various ways you can promote your online business and make effective use of your online marketing budgets. Build a comprehensive internet marketing strategy complete with search engine optimization, a user-friendly company website, thought leadership articles and blogs, as well as a dynamic social media presence. Be confident in your business and your products and services!

A final example of how social media can affect brands:
Consumer products giant Procter & Gamble (P&G) has a considerable social media presence and the company's businesses all have their dedicated online communities. Its feminine care group built an online community called Beinggirl as a destination for teenage girls to seek and share information about feminine health and care. The group sought to make Beinggirl a community, which would provide health information as well as a platform to share the daily, somewhat embarrassing, experiences of teenagers in a safe yet fun environment. The community, by engaging its customer base in helpful and constructive conversations, became a social media engagement success and was soon driving not only huge traffic but also sales.
Recently, however, the brand was at the receiving end of a social media protest. P&G's Pamper product line launched its "revolutionary" Dry Max technology for diapers which offered 20% more absorption but was 20% thinner than its Cruisers line. The company claimed the technology made the new diapers more environmentally

friendly than previous versions. However, Pampers made the mistake of shipping the new diapers in old packaging without clarifying its effects and benefits. Also, it only released the new product in some parts of the United States, with the official release date scheduled months later. To add to their woes, the company had not yet readied any kind of social media campaigns for the product. So when Louisiana mom Rosana Shah, whose child had developed diaper rash, began a Facebook page to force the company to withdraw the product, other parents joined in with their stories of rashes and blisters. By May 7,000 parents had joined Shah's campaign. Stung by the online response, the company quickly compensated some complaining parents – and immediately took to social media networks to explain the new product and set up a Facebook FAQ page to answer queries from parents.

**Stick to the basics**
Companies that benefit from social media reputation strategies are those that consistently deliver the promised service or results. Delivering results builds trust. Never lose sight of the fundamentals while dealing with social media avenues. Allow yourself to be guided by your brand values in all your social media interactions. All your social media actions and conversations must be authentic and relevant to your customers and community members. Don't preach; Entertain. Remember, Blendtec's "Will it blend" YouTube clips in which the company's CEO Tom Dickson blended various non-food items in Blendtec blenders? Since its launch, the videos have been viewed over 100 million times and sales have seen an increase of over 700%.

The key, of course, is to never take your eyes off your customers' requirements. Take advantage of social media opportunities to firstly, know and understand your customers rather than jumping into 'sell' mode right away. You can utilize the instant reach of social media to enhance your brand reputation as well as to conduct immediate damage control if such an occasion arises. Beware of making the rules in any social media conversations – it's the participants who moderate social media communities and as a business owner, you and your employees must be alert to these rules of engagement. One rule of thumb – Do not say or do anything that you do not want to see published in a newspaper!

If small business owners can exploit the available social media opportunities while maintaining their brand promise and are willing to adapt themselves to the changing pace of social media developments – well, you are well on your way to succeed!

Fergus Boyd, Virgin Atlantic Airways' head of e-business, has been quoted as saying, "Twitter is no more than a sound bite. Facebook can be an article. The website is for in-depth detail. They all need to signpost each other."

# References

1to1 Media.com
1729.com

## A
All Facebook.com
AccuraCast News
Ahren.org
AimClear Blog
AME Info.com
AppBoy.com

## B
BBC.co.uk
BetterNetworker.com
Best Social Media Marketing  BlogHerald.com
BoardReader.com
Brian Solis.com
Brick Marketing.com
Business Week Online Magazine
Business BlogConsulting.com

## C
CBS Business Network
Chris Brogan.com
CIO.com
Connect.icrossing.co.uk
CopyBlogger.com
Co.mments.com
CRM Advocate
CRM Today.com
CrunchBase.com
Customer Think Blog.com
CurbsideCupcakes

## D
David Pierce; LostinTechnology.com
Denise Wakeman; Build a Better Blog.com
Destination CRM.com
Deuts.blogspot.com
Direct2Dell Blog
Doshdosh.com
Doug Williams; WebDesignSEO.com
Duct Tape Marketing Blog
Dustin Brewer.com

## E
Erica O'Grady on Blog of Mr Tweet
Evan Bartlett.com
Eventslisted.com
Extanz.com

## F
Facebook Insights
FindandConvert.com
Filtrbox.com
Flickr.com
Flyte.biz
Foursquare.com
Fusion Brand Blogs
FutureLab.net Blog
Future Buzz.com

## G
Gigaom.com
Google Analytics
Google Support
Google Website Optimizer
Gowalla.com
GrubStreet San Francisco Food News
Guerrilla Freelancing.com

**H**
Hootsuite.com
HubPages.com
HubSpotBlog.com
Hugo Guzman.com

**I**
IBM.com
Icerocket.com
ICPUG.org.uk
iMediaConnection.com
InsideFacebook.com
InfoWorld.com
InvesPBlog.com

**J**
Jeff Jarvis; BuzzMachine.com

**K**
Keotag.com

**L**
Laser Burn Media.com
LinkBuilding.net
LinkedIn.com
LovesThreadLess.com
Lucy Beer; WebTrainingWheels.com

**M**
MarketingVox.com
Marketing-Jive.com
Mashable.com
Maisha Walker; INC.com
McKinseyQuarterly.com
MediaNeedle.com
MMetrics.com
MissionPie.com
MPDailyfix.com

## N
National Law Review
NYTimes.com

## O
OgilvyPR.com
Omniture's SiteCatalyst
Optimizely.com

## P
Penn State University News Playfish.com
PrevailPR.com
PublicRelationsBlogger.com

## R
Rafe Needleman; CNET news
RajAnand.biz
Reel SEO Blogs
Romow.com

## S
Scout Blogging.com
SearchEnginePeople.com
SearchEngineLand.com
Search Engine Guide.com
Search Engine Journal.com
Search Cowboys.com
Seibertron.com
SEM Insights.com
SEO Blog on User Personas
SEO.com
SEOmoz.org
Serph.com
SimplyBusiness.co.uk
Slideshare.net
Slideshare Mobile.net
SmallFuel.com
Small Business SEM.com
Small Business Newz.com
Smashing Magazine.com

SMBTrendwire.com
Social Media Today.com
SocialMediaExaminer.com
SocialTimes.com
Socialized PR Blog
SocialMention.com
Stay on Search.com

## T
Tips.com
TheWWWBlog.com
TopRankBlog.com
Tech-Recipes.com
Twitter 101
Twitter Blog
TweetDeck.com
Twitter.com
Tweetbeep.com
Technorati.com
TechCrunch.com
Trendrr.com
Tweetmeme.com
Twitter Counter.com

## V
Viral Heat.com
Visual Website Optimizer

## W
WebSolutions.com
WebCredible.co.uk
WebworkerDaily.com
WordPress blog stats
WSI e-Services.com
Windmill Networking

## Y
YackTrack.com
Yahoo Videos
Yahoo.com

Yelp.com
YouTube Blog

# Z
Zynga.com

# Bibliography

1to1 Media.com
1729.com

## A
All Facebook.com
AccuraCast News
Ahren.org
AimClear Blog
AME Info.com
AppBoy.com

## B
BBC.co.uk
BetterNetworker.com
Best Social Media Marketing
BlogHerald.com
BoardReader.com
Brian Solis.com
Brick Marketing.com
Business Week Online Magazine
Business BlogConsulting.com

## C
CBS Business Network
Chris Brogan.com
CIO.com
Co.mments.com
ComputerWeekly.com
Connect.icrossing.co.uk
CopyBlogger.com
CRM Advocate
CRM Today.com
CrunchBase.com
Customer Think Blog.com
CurbsideCupcakes.com

**D**
David Pierce; LostinTechnology.com
Denise Wakeman; Build a Better Blog.com
Destination CRM.com
Deuts.blogspot.com
Direct2Dell Blog
Doshdosh.com
Doug Williams; WebDesignSEO.com
Duct Tape Marketing Blog
Dustin Brewer.com

**E**
Economist.com
eMarketer.com
Erica O'Grady on Blog of Mr Tweet
Evan Bartlett.com
Eventslisted.com
Extanz.com

**F**
Facebook Insights
FindandConvert.com
Filtrbox.com
Flickr.com
Flyte.biz
Foursquare.com
Fusion Brand Blogs
FutureLab.net Blog
Future Buzz.com

**G**
Gigaom.com
Google Analytics
Google Support
Google Website Optimizer
Gowalla.com
GrubStreet San Francisco Food News
Guerrilla Freelancing.com

## H
Hootsuite.com
HubPages.com
HubSpotBlog.com
Hugo Guzman.com

## I
IBM.com
Icerocket.com
ICPUG.org.uk
iMediaConnection.com
InsideFacebook.com
InfoWorld.com
InvesPBlog.com

## J
Jeff Jarvis; BuzzMachine.com

## K
Keotag.com

## L
Laser Burn Media.com
LATimes.com
LinkBuilding.net
LinkedIn.com
LovesThreadLess.com
Lucy Beer; WebTrainingWheels.com

## M
MarketingVox.com
Marketing-Jive.com
Mashable.com
Maisha Walker; INC.com
McKinseyQuarterly.com
MediaNeedle.com
MMetrics.com
MissionPie.com
MPDailyfix.com

**N**
National Law Review
Nielsen.com
NYTimes.com

**O**
OgilvyPR.com
Omniture's SiteCatalyst
OpenForum.com
Optimizely.com

**P**
Penn State University News Playfish.com
PrevailPR.com
PublicRelationsBlogger.com

**R**
Rafe Needleman; CNET news
RajAnand.biz
Reel SEO Blogs
Romow.com

**S**
Salesforce.com
Scout Blogging.com
SearchEnginePeople.com
SearchEngineLand.com
Search Engine Guide.com
Search Engine Journal.com
Search Cowboys.com
Seibertron.com
SEM Insights.com
SEO Blog on User Personas
SEO.com
SEOmoz.org
Serph.com
SimplyBusiness.co.uk
Slideshare.net
Slideshare Mobile.net
SmallFuel.com

Small Business SEM.com
Small Business Newz.com
Smashing Magazine.com
SMBTrendwire.com
Social Media Today.com
SocialMediaExaminer.com
SocialTimes.com
Socialized PR Blog
SocialMention.com
Stay on Search.com

## T
Tips.com
TheWWWBlog.com
TopRankBlog.com
Tech-Recipes.com
Twitter 101
Twitter Blog
TweetDeck.com
Twitter.com
Tweetbeep.com
Technorati.com
TechCrunch.com
Trendrr.com
Tweetmeme.com
Twitter Counter.com

## V
Viral Heat.com
Visual Website Optimizer

## W
WebSolutions.com
WebCredible.co.uk
WebworkerDaily.com
WordPress blog stats
WSI e-Services.com
Windmill Networking

**Y**
YackTrack.com
Yahoo Videos
Yahoo.com
Yelp.com
YouTube Blog

**Z**
Zynga.com

# Links Index

http://ahren.org/code/bit/posterous-a-critical-look
http://appboy.com/android/seesmic-for-android-56516/
http://articles.latimes.com/2009/feb/11/food/fo-kogi11
http://biz.yelp.com/
http://blog.hubspot.com/blog/tabid/6307/bid/5079/6-Social-Media-Marketing-Case-Study-Lessons.aspx#ixzz0orFEq9qP
http://blog.linkedin.com/category/success-stories/
http://blog.mrtweet.com/twitter-to-go-how-one-local-coffee-shop-used-twitter-to-double-his-clientele
http://blog.ogilvypr.com/2008/10/the-twitter-strategy-blog-series-post-1-customer-relations/
http://blog.twitter.com/2010/04/twitter-for-iphone.html
http://boardreader.com/
http://boardtracker.com/
http://bx.businessweek.com/social-media-business-failures/6-common-linkedin-mistakes-small-businesses-make-and-what-you-should-do-instead—technology—american-express-open-forum/15578287973947855721-1314b39cceff867f204107ad508e82e5/
http://co.mments.com/login
http://collecta.com/
http://connect.icrossing.co.uk/twitter_1637
http://deuts.blogspot.com/2009/05/microblogging-tumblr-vs-posterous.html
http://dustinbrewer.com/top-10-reasons-you-should-be-using-linkedin/
http://en.community.dell.com/dell-blogs/Direct2Dell/b/direct2dell/archive/2009/12/08/expanding-connections-with-customers-through-social-media.aspx
http://en.wikipedia.org/wiki/BlackPlanet
http://en.wikipedia.org/wiki/Classmates.com
http://en.wikipedia.org/wiki/LinkedIn#Features
http://en.wikipedia.org/wiki/LiveJournal
http://en.wikipedia.org/wiki/MiGente.com
http://en.wikipedia.org/wiki/Online_reputation_management
http://en.wikipedia.org/wiki/Search_engine_optimization
http://en.wikipedia.org/wiki/Tumblr
http://en.wikipedia.org/wiki/World_Wide_Web
http://en.wikipedia.org/wiki/Yahoo!_Answers
http://entrepreneurs.about.com/b/2008/04/29/managing-unprofitable-customers.htm
http://eu.techcrunch.com/2010/07/23/reviewpro-releases-a-free-reputation-management-tool-for-concerne-hoteliers/
http://evbart.com/2009/05/anatomy-of-a-failed-twitter-campaign/
http://extanz.com/2010/05/03/social-media-rules-what-nestle-forgot/
http://ezinearticles.com/

http://ezinearticles.com/?How-to-Market-Your-Blog-Successfully&id=3557334http://foursquare.com/businesses/
http://ezinearticles.com/?Internet-Marketing-Strategies---6-Top-Facebook-Marketing-Strategies&id=4199695
http://ezinearticles.com/?Internet-Marketing-Strategies---6-Top-Facebook-Marketing-Strategies&id=4199695
http://ezinearticles.com/?Learn-How-to-Keep-Track-of-Your-Video-Statistics&id=4484128
http://flickr.com/
http://fusionbrand.blogs.com/fusionbrand/2004/07/what_to_do_abou.html
http://gowalla.com/
http://hbr.org/2008/04/the-right-way-to-manage-unprofitable-customers/ar/1
http://help.yahoo.com/l/us/yahoo/answers/abuse/guidelines-10.html
http://hootsuite.com/
http://hubpages.com/hub/How-YouTube-Can-Make-You-Money---The-Lauren-Luke-Success-Story
http://inventors.about.com/library/weekly/aa091598.htm
http://inventors.about.com/od/istartinventions/a/internet.htm
http://lajuett.blogspot.com/2010/03/did-i-mention-social-media.html
http://learn.linkedin.com/profiles/
http://linkbuilding.net/2010/06/10/never-trip-in-link-building-with-stumbleupon-2/
http://live.psu.edu/story/41446
http://m.slideshare.com/
http://marketingpr.suite101.com/article.cfm/online-video-marketing-tips-for-small-businesses
http://mashable.com/2008/03/11/online-reputation/
http://mashable.com/2008/03/26/youtube-insights/
http://mashable.com/2008/06/05/social-media-strategy/
http://mashable.com/2008/11/02/force-sites/
http://mashable.com/2008/12/24/free-brand-monitoring-tools/
http://mashable.com/2008/12/29/brand-reputation-monitoring-tools/
http://mashable.com/2009/01/21/best-twitter-brands/
http://mashable.com/2009/02/06/social-media-smartest-brands/
http://mashable.com/2009/02/07/twitter-clients/
http://mashable.com/2009/02/12/personal-branding-102/
http://mashable.com/2009/03/27/cotweet/
http://mashable.com/2009/04/15/social-media-seo/
http://mashable.com/2009/05/13/facebook-brand-apps/
http://mashable.com/2009/05/27/facebook-page-vs-group/
http://mashable.com/2009/07/27/linkedin-personal-brand/
http://mashable.com/2009/08/03/linkedin-company-profile/
http://mashable.com/2009/09/04/twitter-hashtags-business/
http://mashable.com/2009/09/21/business-blogging-mistakes/
http://mashable.com/2009/09/22/facebook-pages-guide/
http://mashable.com/2009/09/22/social-media-business/

http://mashable.com/2009/10/12/social-media-pr-pitch/
http://mashable.com/2009/10/21/social-media-small-businesses/
http://mashable.com/2009/10/28/small-business-marketing/
http://mashable.com/2010/02/17/social-media-attention/
http://mashable.com/2010/03/22/small-business-social-media-results/
http://mashable.com/2010/04/08/managing-online-reputation/
http://mashable.com/2010/04/22/mobile-social-networking-2/
http://mashable.com/2010/04/23/youtube-small-business/
http://mashable.com/2010/04/30/twitter-ad-model-small-business/
http://mashable.com/2010/05/21/social-crm/
http://mashable.com/2010/05/21/surprising-social-media-business-success/
http://mashable.com/2010/06/02/small-business-social-media-success-stories/
http://mashable.com/2010/10/21/social-media-management-tools/
http://mashable.com/tag/salesforcecom/
http://mmetrics.com/fre/Press_Events/Press_Releases/2008/03/iPhone_Hype_Holds_Up
http://moblogsmoproblems.blogspot.com/2007/05/company-blog-checkup-kodak.html
http://news.bbc.co.uk/2/hi/uk_news/8116869.stm
http://news.cnet.com/8301-19882_3-10457332-250.html
http://pizzaseo.com/user-personas-testing
http://press.linkedin.com/IrishStartup
http://press.linkedin.com/success-stories
http://prevailpr.com/how-to-25-twitter-strategies-to-improve-your-business
http://publicrelationsblogger.com/search/label/Public%20Relations%20and%20Social%2
   Media
http://rajanand.biz/2009/11/09/social-media-for-recruitment-case-study-ernst-young/
http://sanfrancisco.grubstreet.com/2010/12/mission_pies_karen_heisler_and.html
http://sbinformation.about.com/cs/ecommerce/a/bblogs.htm
http://search.twitter.com/search?q=uftradiochat
http://searchengineland.com/3-ways-social-media-marketing-helps-seo-10715
http://searchengineland.com/25-tips-to-optimize-your-blog-for-readers-search
   engines-10226
http://searchengineland.com/a-small-business-marketing-success-story-john-tuggle-guitar
   teacher-13746
http://searchengineland.com/social-media-and-seo-16643
http://seminsights.com/opinions/seo-success-stories
http://smallhomebusiness.suite101.com/article.cfm/facebook_for_small_business_owners
http://socialmention.com/
Suite101.com
http://support.tweetdeck.com/entries/129001-what-s-new-in-tweetdeck-v0-34
http://techcrunch.com/2009/05/02/how-to-grow-your-blog-through-customer-development/
http://techcrunch.com/2010/07/17/how-social-media-drives-new-business-six-case-studies/
http://thefuturebuzz.com/2008/06/03/case-study-building-buzz-blogosphere-joffreys-coffee/
http://thefuturebuzz.com/2009/08/19/social-seo-strategy/
http://tweetbeep.com/

http://tweetmeme.com/
https://twitter.com/twitter101/case_bestbuy
https://twitter.com/twitter101/case_coffeegroundz
https://twitter.com/twitter101/case_jetblue
http://twittercounter.com/
http://video.yahoo.com/watch/7107569/18497813
http://visualwebsiteoptimizer.com/case-studies.php
http://weblogs.hitwise.com/us-heather-hopkins/2007/12/knol_numbers_to_lend_context_t html
http://websearch.about.com/od/keywordsandphrases/a/blogseo.htm
http://websiteoptimizer.blogspot.com/2009/04/landing-page-testing-with-offline.html
http://websiteoptimizer.blogspot.com/2010/02/25-google-website-optimizer-tips-for.html
http://websiteoptimizer.blogspot.com/2010/02/how-to-quadruple-conversion-rate.html
http://webworkerdaily.com/2009/06/16/real-life-twitter-business-success-stories/
http://webworkerdaily.com/2009/07/13/33-ways-to-use-linkedin-for-business/
http://windmillnetworking.com/2009/04/27/how-do-i-set-up-a-company-profile-on linkedin/#axzz0r2DxumGi
http://windmillnetworking.com/2009/08/11/linkedin-profile-tips-the-10-mistakes-you-want-to avoid-and-why/
http://wordpress.org/extend/plugins/stats/
http://www.tech-recipes.com/rx/1064/how-to-market-your-blog-and-keep-your-readers/
http://www.thewwwblog.com/why-wordpress-is-better-than-blogger.html
http://www.toprankblog.com/2006/06/25-tips-for-marketing-your-blog/
http://www.toprankblog.com/2007/01/seo-benefits-from-blogs/
http://www.tourismkeys.ca/blog/2008/10/6-twitter-strategies-for-building-your-brand/
http://www.webcredible.co.uk/user-friendly-resources/search-engine-optimisation/number-links.shtml
http://www.webtrainingwheels.com/2010/03/9-reasons-why-hootsuite-is-the-best-twitter tool/
http://www.wsieservices.be/_blog/Marketing_on_Internet_Road/post/Why_LinkedIn_is Important_to_your_Business/
http://www-01.ibm.com/software/lotus/products/connections/features.html
http://www.1729.com/blog/NewFormOfAdvertisingTransparentPaidReviews.html
http://www.1to1media.com/view.aspx?docid=31900
http://www.accuracast.com/search-daily-news/social-media-7471/innovative-ikea campaign/
http://www.allfacebook.com/2009/07/facebook-small-business/
http://www.aimclearblog.com/2009/06/09/4-video-optimization-experts-dish-killer-tips/
http://www.ameinfo.com/16743.html
http://www.bestsocialmediamarketingtips.com/3492
http://www.betternetworker.com/articles/view/marketing/social-content/top-twitter-apps-by mashable-and-the-ratings
http://www.bizreport.com/2010/04/report_social_media_increases_intent_to_purchase.html
http://www.blogherald.com/2007/12/28/top-10-ways-to-market-your-blog-in-2008/

http://www.bnet.com/cp/the-right-way-to-manage-unprofitable-customers/197382
http://www.briansolis.com/2010/02/roi-how-to-measure-return-on-investment-in-social media/
http://www.brickmarketing.com/what-is-reputation-management.htm
http://www.buildabetterblog.com/2009/01/backtype-helps.html
http://www.businessblogconsulting.com/2004/12/business_blog_c
http://www.businessweek.com/bwdaily/dnflash/content/oct2007/db20071017_277576.htm
http://www.capturecommerce.com/automotive-case-study.php
http://www.chrisbrogan.com/50-ideas-on-using-twitter-for-business/
http://www.chrisbrogan.com/make-your-linkedin-profile-work-for-you/
http://www.cio.com/article/492611/LinkedIn_Profiles_Avoid_the_Six_Most_Common Mistakes
http://www.computerweekly.com/Articles/2009/03/17/235284/SMEs-use-Twitter-to-cut costs.htm
http://www.copyblogger.com/grow-business-twitter/
http://www.crm2day.com/editorial/EpyApyupVypDxknGnC.php
http://www.crunchbase.com/company/classmates-com
http://www.customerthink.com/blog/southwest_airlines_vs_kevin_smith_a_case_study_in customer_experience_and_social_media
http://www.davesite.com/webstation/net-history1.shtml
http://www.destinationcrm.com/Articles/CRM-News/Daily-News/Predictive-Analytics-Can Pinpoint-Profitable-Customers-52164.aspx
http://www.doshdosh.com/a-comprehensive-guide-to-stumbleupon-how-to-build-massive-traffic-to-your-website-and-monetize-it/
http://www.doshdosh.com/how-to-become-a-top-stumbleupon-user-or-why-shouldnt-bother/
http://www.ducttapemarketing.com/blog/2009/01/20/explore-the-twitter-hashtag/
http://www.economist.com/node/15350960
http://www.economist.com/node/15351002?story_id=15351002
http://www.eventslisted.com/eventlaunchstrategies/new-media/strategies/quantity-vs quality-debate
http://www.facebook.com/help/?search=insights#!/help/?page=1103
http://www.filtrbox.com/
http://www.findandconvert.com/blog/
http://www.flotzam.com/archivist/
http://www.flyte.biz/resources/newsletters/08/12-facebook-for-small-business.php
http://www.futurelab.net/blogs/marketing-strategy-innovation/2009/05/the_five_archetypal business_t.html
http://www.google.com/analytics/
http://www.google.com/support/websiteoptimizer/bin/answer.py?hl=en&answer=55894
http://www.google.com/support/websiteoptimizer/bin/answer.py?hl=en&answer=55895
http://www.google.com/support/websiteoptimizer/bin/answer.py?hl=en&answer=55898
http://www.google.com/websiteoptimizer/workout/index.html
http://www.google.com/support/youtube/bin/answer.py?hl=en&answer=147619
http://www.guerrillafreelancing.com/the-10-biggest-mistakes-people-make-on-stumble-upon/

http://www.guruofsearch.com/advantages-google-analytics
http://www.hugoguzman.com/2010/07/looking-clear-cut-social-media-roi-theres-an-seo-for-that/
http://www.icerocket.com/
http://www.icpug.org.uk/national/features/040105fe.htm
http://www.imediaconnection.com/content/23240.asp
http://www.inc.com/maisha-walker/2009/08/linkedin_small_business_success.html
http://www.inc.com/maisha-walker/2009/09/building_your_tribe_-_6_linked3.html
http://www.infoworld.com/t/networking/social-enterprise-036
http://www.insidefacebook.com/2007/12/09/inside-facebook-marketing-bible-24-ways-to-market-your-brand-company-product-or-service-in-facebook/
http://www.insidefacebook.com/2010/03/22/levis-sees-early-traction-with-live-music-driven-facebook-campaign/
http://www.invesp.com/blog/ecommerce/personas-can-ecommerce-do-without-them.html
http://www.invesp.com/blog/sales-marketing/discover-the-three-essentail-design-factors-to-improve-online-conversion-rate.html
http://www.jeffthomascobb.com/2010/01/facebook-small-business-success-stories/
http://www.jeffthomascobb.com/2010/03/facebook-fan-page-tips/
http://www.keotag.com/
http://www.laserburnmedia.com/2010/05/10/5-ways-social-media-can-hurt-your-business/
http://www.linkedin.com/answers/marketing-sales/business-development/MAR BDV/741477-10170136
http://www.linkedin.com/answers/professional-development/communication-public speaking/PRO_COM/603151-4779
http://www.lostintechnology.com/internet-tools/5-great-alternatives-to-the-twitter-interface
http://www.lovesthreadless.com/
http://www.mangoorange.com/2010/05/24/social-media-free-facebook-marketing-strategies/
http://www.marketing-jive.com/2008/01/optimizing-for-blended-search-what-you.html
http://www.marketingvox.com/dominos-employees-cause-youtube-brand-scandal-043809/
http://www.mckinseyquarterly.com/Marketing/Strategy/A_new_way_to_measure_word-of mouth_marketing_2567?gp=1
http://www.medianeedle.com/blog/2010/01/buzz-in-a-vacuum-transparency-in-social media-marketing/
http://www.mpdailyfix.com/how-should-your-company-handle-negative-blog-comments/
http://www.natlawreview.com/article/lawyers-and-linkedin-lawyers-and-linkedin-success stories-cautions-and-small-complaint
http://www.newsweek.com/id/187008
http://www.nielsen.com/us/en/insights/events-webinars/2010/understanding-the-value-of-a-social-media-impression.html
http://www.nytimes.com/2009/07/23/business/smallbusiness/23twitter.html
http://www.omniture.com/en/products/online_analytics/sitecatalyst
http://www.oneriot.com/

http://www.openforum.com/idea-hub/topics/technology/article/how-social-media-helps-one-small-business-connect-with-fans-leah-betancourt
http://www.optimizely.com/whatisabtesting
www.playfish.com
http://www.readwriteweb.com/archives/social_media_crm_what_are_rules_of_engagement.php
http://www.realmarket.com/required/sedonacorp2.pdf
http://www.reelseo.com/types-online-video-business/
http://www.romow.com/internet-blog/blog-comment-marketing-to-gain-traffic/
http://www.romow.com/internet-blog/keep-track-of-your-online-conversations-and-blog-comments/
http://www.salesforce.com/chatter/whatischatter/
http://www.scobleizer.com/
http://www.scoutblogging.com/tips.html
http://www.search.twitter.com/
http://www.searchcowboys.com/columns/1528
http://www.searchengineguide.com/kimberly-krause-berg/my-first-user-persona.php
http://www.searchengineguide.com/manoj-jasra/leveraging-facebook-groups.php
http://www.searchenginejournal.com/blended-search-how-b2b-companies-can-benefit/6992/
http://www.searchenginejournal.com/seo-blogging-success-story-diabetes-blog-earns-40k-per-year/5240/
http://www.searchenginepeople.com/blog/most-effective-ways-to-search-and-track-online-conversations.html
http://www.seibertron.com/energonpub/viewtopic.php?f=14&t=58408
http://www.seo.com/blog/using-linkedin-for-seo/
http://www.seomoz.org/blog/21-tactics-to-increase-blog-traffic
http://www.seomoz.org/blog/creating-online-video-strategy
http://www.serph.com/
http://www.simplybusiness.co.uk/knowledge/articles/2010/04/2010-04-23-four-social-media-marketing-disasters/
http://www.slideshare.net/aspoeth/twitter-words-presentation
http://www.slideshare.net/customersforever/optimizing-your-organizations-ability-to-get-keep-grow-customers
http://www.slideshare.net/PingElizabeth/social-media-lessons-from-the-obama-campaign
http://www.slideshare.net/whitehouse
http://www.smallbusinesssem.com/a-guide-to-social-marketing-on-yahoo-answers/1056/
http://www.smallbusinessnewz.com/topnews/2010/04/21/report-most-small-businesses-still-not-sold-on-social-media
http://www.smallfuel.com/blog/entry/how-to-leverage-twitter-for-your-business
http://www.smashingmagazine.com/2009/06/03/9-crucial-ui-features-of-social-media-and-networking-sites/
http://www.smbtrendwire.com/using-facebook-small-business/
http://www.socializedpr.com/youtube-might-not-be-best-place-for-corporate-social-media/

http://www.socialmediaexaminer.com/five-facebook-only-strategies-for-business-success/
http://www.socialmediatoday.com/SMC/121162
http://www.socialmediatoday.com/SMC/179998
http://www.socialmediatoday.com/SMC/23009
http://www.socialtimes.com/2010/02/social-media-metrics/
http://www.squidoo.com/5-conversion-optimization
http://www.stayonsearch.com/how-to-increase-your-revenue-by-retaining-customers
http://www.tealium.com/products/social-media/index.html
http://www.technorati.com/
http://www.techrigy.com/
http://www.toprankblog.com/2009/04/seo-social-media-roadmap/
http://www.trendrr.com/
http://www.twazzup.com/
http://www.viralheat.com/
http://www.webdesignseo.com/web-design/user-persona-a-tool-to-increase-conversion.php
http://www.websolutions.com/Blog/BlogView.asp?BlogID=4096819
http://www.womenhomebusiness.com/success/curbsidecupcakes-com-success-in-using social-media.htm
http://www.yacktrack.com/
http://www.yelp.com/business/review_response
www.zynga.com
http://youtube-global.blogspot.com/2008/03/youtube-reveals-video-analytics-tool.html

Sales 3.0 The New Cont@ct Sport™

# Quick Order Form

**Telephone Orders**: Call 847-359-6969
Have your credit card ready.

**Email Orders**: doug@dougdvorak.com

**Postal Orders**: DMG, Inc.
Doug Dvorak
311 Village Drive PMB 3167
Donnelly, ID 83615, USA
Telephone: 847-359-6969

**Please send the following books**. I understand that I may return any of them for a full refund ☐ for any reason, no questions asked.

_____
_____
_____

**Please send more FREE information on**:

☐ Other Books          ☐ Speaking/Seminars          ☐ Consulting

Name: _____
Address: _____
City: _____ State: _____ Zip: _____
Telephone _____
Email address: _____

**Sales tax**: Please add 9.75% for products shipped to Illinois addresses.

**Shipping by air**

**US**: $5.00 for first book and $2.00 for each additional product.

**International**: $9.00 for first book; $5.00 for each additional product (estimate).

# Quick Order Form

**Telephone Orders**: Call 847-359-6969
Have your credit card ready.

**Email Orders**: doug@dougdvorak.com

**Postal Orders**: DMG, Inc.
Doug Dvorak
311 Village Drive PMB 3167
Donnelly, ID 83615, USA
Telephone: 847-359-6969

**Please send the following books**. I understand that I may return any of them for a full refund ☐ for any reason, no questions asked.

_____
_____
_____

**Please send more FREE information on**:

☐ Other Books     ☐ Speaking/Seminars     ☐ Consulting

Name: _____
Address: _____
City: _____ State: _____ Zip: _____
Telephone _____
Email address: _____

**Sales tax**: Please add 9.75% for products shipped to Illinois addresses.

**Shipping by air**

**US**: $5.00 for first book and $2.00 for each additional product.

**International**: $9.00 for first book; $5.00 for each additional product (estimate).

# Sales 3.0
## The New Cont@ct Sport™

For Information on Doug's
Social Media Marketing Workshops,
Keynote Presentations and
Consulting Services
Call (847) 359 6969 or
Email doug@dougdvorak.com
www.newcontactsport.com

www.ingramcontent.com/pod-product-compliance
Lightning Source LLC
Chambersburg PA
CBHW051642170526
45167CB00001B/295